TABLE FOR ONE

Intro: Trying to cram 40 years of memories into one book is like trying to cram a 48 inch body into a size 38 inch suit. You have to figure out the best way to cut it and tailor so it will fit without damaging it too much. Think of me as the tailor of this collection of memories. I would like to thank my wife Robbie for supporting me and editing this volume of stories. I also wish to thank all the folks I have worked with along the way, and last but not least, the families that we served. Special thanks go to Dennis Nilson, my embalmer and friend of 42 years.

Prologue

** "Who is that guy mopping the entryway?" This question was asked by one embalmer to another at the funeral parlor that I was soon to learn was everything but funereal. My name is Don Lee. A little name for such a big guy. After getting my BA in Political Science from MU and serving a couple months as a CNA at a local hospital, I quickly realized that BA plus MU equaled CNA for me in 1978.**

** One of the lawns I mowed in my spare time for spending money belonged to the owner of the local mortuary. Wanting to better myself and having grown up with a morbid curiosity as to exactly what went on in the basement of such a place at night, I asked the old gentleman if he needed any help at the funeral parlor. This inquiry led me to 5 decades in the funeral business and provides the body of work that follows. Get comfortable. I promise chapters short on length but long on insights into people. Living and dead. You will go with me on death calls. You will walk the creaking halls of the funeral parlor at all hours of the day and night. You will witness people behaving both good and bad during the worst time of their life. You will enter the intimate scenes of deaths both expected and unexpected. You don't need a suit and tie. Just bring your own morbid curiosity**

1

and a quest for a peek behind the scenes of one of the most feared and misunderstood ways to make a living.

I was fortunate enough to serve in this profession during the years when funerals were a means to honor a life well lived rather than simply dispose of the remains. Let's start at the beginning, shall we?

A Grave Undertaking

Old Charlie, the owner of the local funeral parlor, had hired me on a trial basis. He asked me to dig a grave and would reward me with fifty bucks. Mt. Zion Cemetery in early February was indeed cold as a grave digger's behind. Here is another caveat about my book of cadavers. Your child can read it, your mother can read, yes even your pastor can read it because it will be like an empty hen house. No foul language here. I will substitute suitable and genteel words in place of gratuitous exclamations of bad language.

Hand digging a grave when the ground is frozen to a depth of 10 inches requires a pick axe to chop through the clay. Then digging a hole 7 foot long by 3 and a half foot wide and 5 foot deep takes time and strenuous back-breaking labor. I recruited my dad and brother-in-law. We worked 4 hours that Saturday afternoon and finally completed the excavation by dark. Charlie offered to run and get us a sandwich, even inquiring about our preferences. Forty-one years later I am still waiting for that sandwich. The next afternoon after a mercifully brief graveside service, the guest of honor was lowered into the tundral abyss. Luckily, the family had left for a warmer clime when my tobacco pipe slipped out of my overall bib and into the grave as we were filling it in. The pipe was retrieved, and we took the fake grass and tent back to the ancient storage building located in the bowels of Columbia Cemetery. We arrived there about dusk. Our plans to spook each other were aborted by the extreme cold.

And darkness. Six hours labor times 3 guys equal 18 man hours. I believe we made about $2.77 an hour. It was my first and last time digging a grave. The experience did get my foot in the door, though. Charlie hired me to assist at the parlor but forgot to tell anyone else, including the other employees or his partners.

Check That Toilet

Monday morning I wanted to make a good impression and pulled into the parking garage promptly at 7:30 AM. I was getting out of my 76 GMC pickup when an angry-looking, middle-aged man accosted me. "You can't park that sunova blank there!" I was equally dismayed by his rudeness and the speech impediment that made his statement sound like, "Huhyew cant park that hummich oer dere." I was tempted to honor the flight part of the fight or flight equation, but I needed the job. I informed Don (He shared my name) that I work there and was told by Charlie to park there. I went in and grabbed a mop to appear busy and make a good impression. Two embalmers were at the front door smoking and discussing current events when they spied me. I was just about finished mopping when Don came running up and bellered, "What the (impeded sounding curse) are you doing, Don Lee?"
I managed a weak, "Huh?" He spat out, "Tryin to make us look bad? We don't do that here or they will expect us to do that again. Got it?"
He then ended the encounter with an explosive release of flatulence as he giggled and walked off. He then appeared with a pair of pliers and said the toilet in the ladies' restroom required some maintenance. He got very specific and explained the problem was near the floor behind the stool. As I was bending down, I heard the door slam shut. Then as the wave of stench encompassed me, I pushed desperately at a door that was

wedged shut with a funeral home folding chair placed strategically under the door knob.

I was to find out later that the elderly female partner of the parlor used this particular toilet because of its remote site to perform her daily morning bowel movement. The combination of the whiskey toddy she took each night and her morning breakfast of egg was enough to create what was commonly referred to as "the wildcat." She let the wildcat out every morning, and it became an integral part of my hazing and welcome to the funeral parlor.

Bump Juice

In early 1978, I was anxious to satisfy my curiosity about what went on in the mysterious locked room in the back of the building. The entrance to the hallway containing the forbidden room was located in an alley in the old business part of town.

Back in those days the "loved one," never to be referred to as a body or corpse or stiff, was transported from the place of death to the funeral home in an actual hearse. The hearse was always referred to as a funeral coach. It was always a production to stop the traffic on Walnut street so you could back the hearse down the alley.

A couple of days into my new job, one of the embalmers named "Greg" lured me into the prep room or morgue with the promise of showing me exactly what went on back there. I entered the room with a mixture of fear and wonder. Wonder won. I gazed at the body on the table. Greg pulled back the hospital sheet covering the body, and I looked, then looked again. He was covered head to toe in bumps. I mean hideous welts that conjured up thoughts of a full body hornet attack. "What happened to that poor guy?" I questioned. Greg informed me that the unfortunate fellow had entered the hospital for a routine yearly check up and was released 2 days later to the custody of the funeral home.

I watched in awe as Greg made an incision to raise the carotid artery so he could inject the Dodge embalming fluid. My eyes were drawn to the blood draining from the vein as the fluid was pumped in. Later I watched in awe as it came time to run the trocar, a large hollow instrument with a sharp arrow-like tip, into the chest cavity so he could aspirate all the vital organs and drain them. He then used the trocar to inject the cavity fluid. I was so engrossed I didn't notice when Greg detached the trocar from its tubing, "Greg? Is whatever this guy died from contagious?" I asked as I was pondering the sad ending to this guy's life and mentally crossing THAT hospital off my list of potential medical care.

"Better hope it's not!" Greg then proceeded to chase me around the table with the trocar. As he brandished the trocar, he threatened to infect me with "bump juice." I could hear him cackling as I ran from the room and sought refuge from the demented undertaker. What doesn't kill you makes for great stories to tell the grandkids.

Dress Code

Charlie warned me to bring a suit to work in case we received a death call. I was 23 years old and this was the late 1970's. I proudly tucked away my suit and waited for my first call. Just about 1:30 PM that Sunday afternoon one of the embalmers Dennis was napping on one pew in the chapel of the parlor and I was dozing on the other.

The old 2-line phone in the office rang and Dennis took the information. He got off the phone and said, "Get your suit on. Let's roll!" I went up to the "student room" to change. I was so proud of the fact that I had changed and was ready to go in less than 10 minutes that at first I couldn't understand the mirth and outright laughter. Nothing funny here. Someone has died and I am entrusted to take them into our care. Dennis was laughing. At me. Picture a blue denim polyester leisure suit with the pants a couple of inches too short, complimented by a hand-painted purple tie with a green swordfish, that hadn't seen the outside of a closet since my dad had worn it to his wedding 25 years prior. Rounding out the ensemble was a pair of clodhoppers, size 13. In their defense, they were relatively new clodhoppers.

Death calls rarely bring out bullying, but I can still hear the snickers and whispered comments of the nurses as we took the deceased into custody. Well, the next day I was directed to go to JC Penney and get a SUIT. And a tie. And some shoes that did not extend six inches over my ankles.

Triple Ax Murder

I was still green and naive and living at home with my parents. I was put on call every other night and weekend. About 11:30 one night the phone rang. It was the old 10 pound black rotary dial phone located in the hallway. If you grew up in the days before extension phones or cordless phones, you know that those old dinosaurs could roar. BBRRINNG. BBRRINNG. BBRRINNG. Finally, my dad got up and answered the phone. "Don! I think it's the funeral home!" I lumbered sleepily to the phone and half listened until I heard Dennis say, "Multiple fatality ax murder. Get down here now!" As I was struggling to get dressed, I told my dad I was on my way to pick up some ax murder victims. He warned me to be careful as I raced out the door. I sped to the funeral home to find Dennis waiting casually by the hearse. Breathlessly, I asked him how many victims we were going to pick up and if he knew the conditions of the bodies. Decapitation? Limbs missing? Unlimited blood? Where is the scene of the crime?

Dennis grinned and said, "Boone Retirement Center, 85 year old man. Dead in the Bed." No ax murder. No multiple victims. Just an old man. And a relieved junior undertaker. I did learn one thing on that removal, though. In a double room, where both occupants are lying in the supine position, mouth agape, eyes fixed or closed, always listen for snoring and then approach the silent occupant.

Back in the 70's, you could have peace of mind that any time you got a nursing home death it involved a little old lady or little old man. At the time of my retirement, the chances were good that the deceased was closer to 300 pounds than 200. Cots have gotten wider, and caskets have gotten bigger.

Valet Parking

On funeral days, one of my duties was to help park the cars of attendees of the service. The downtown location offered limited parking on the street, so we would take the keys and park cars in the attached parking garage. One elderly gentleman listened politely as I asked him to put the car in park and exit it. He promptly put it in reverse and was attempting to get out when I wrestled it into park before it could drag him and me under it. It was also a good way to diagnose failing brakes.

Another gentleman pulled up and handed me the keys to his pickup. Too late I noticed his "floormat" was a couple of old gunny sacks that he used to spit his tobacco juice into. Saturate one? Simply ease it out and lay another one down.

Charlie had a short-lived suggestion that we clean the windshields on all the cars during the funeral. Why not check the tires and rotate the air in them as well. That suggestion went over like a screen door in a submarine. The garage was heated in the winter but always seemed icy cold most of the time. We finally realized the 3rd partner of the funeral home was quietly shutting the heater off to save money. What really stung was the fact he would grin and get an inordinate amount of joy at our suffering.

I'm not saying the guy was cheap, but he paid cash for a 1975 Ford Fairmont that wasn't even equipped with a radio. He would carry a transistor radio if he were going on a trip. The female partner, Virginia, was equally frugal. She would always step across the street to Ernie's, a popular Columbia restaurant, for her morning coffee around 9 AM. She carried only 26 cents, a quarter and a penny in her hand. No purse or wallet so she wouldn't be in the awkward position of having to buy anyone else's coffee.

Charlie made up for the other two by spending his money freely. He always drove a Cadillac. Those were the golden years of funeral service, and I was too young to realize it. My advice to kids entering any trade today? Soak it up. Enjoy yourself. Make some good memories. Learn from your mistakes. Don't forget God.

Charlie

Charlie was lovable but absent minded. He returned from the car wash one afternoon with a sheepish grin. He needed to borrow some towels from the back to mop out his Caddy because he had left the back windows rolled down. I watched him at a visitation one evening as he patiently listened and listened and then listened some more to a lady intent on telling him something in excruciating detail.
When he was able to break her conversational hold on him he mentioned to me in a stage whisper, "THAT lady could talk your leg off and then whisper up your butt!"

His alcoholic daughter and her son lived with him a couple of blocks from the funeral parlor. He was proud of his skills in being a surrogate father to Billy, his grandson. Billy, all of 14, wanted Charlie to buy him some cigarettes. Charlie offered to purchase him a pouch of tobacco and some rolling papers. "What?" sniffed Billy. "Here you are driving a Cadillac, old man, and you expect me to roll my own smokes??" That'll make a man of him, Charlie explained.

Charlie met his demise in the back alley of the funeral home. He got into a fist fight with his daughter's boyfriend and was knocked to the ground where his head contacted a concrete block. I was given the task to pick him up from the hospital after the autopsy. They were just finishing the autopsy when I entered the morgue in the basement of the Veterans hospital. I told the attendant I was there for Charlie, and he motioned to a table.

Usually the deceased were on a gurney with a covered top that served as camouflage to hide the fact that the attendant was wheeling a body to the morgue. People just saw it and thought it was another load of soiled linen heading to laundry. I looked at the table, and sure enough there was an autopsied body. It really didn't sink in that it indeed was my boss until they peeled his face back over the now empty skull. Yup. That's him.

I drove the flower car to the cemetery for his funeral. I never could understand the logic, but we would always load that van like a pit crew and then speed all the way to the cemetery. We would then set the flowers decoratively around the gravesite making sure to leave them out of the way of the main attraction, the casket. I did my job well and was leaving Grandview Cemetery as I met the procession. A couple of months later, I overheard a long time customer ask Tom, "Hey. Where's Charlie? Haven't seen him around for awhile!" Without missing a beat and with no sign of irony, Tom simply said, "He is working at Grandview today."

Amateur Wrestling

Boys will be boys. Especially a bunch of bored undertakers. Between removals, embalmings, arrangement conferences and funerals, we had quite a bit of idle time. Sometimes the guys would practice their golf swing with putting cups placed around the visitation area. Other times we would wrestle each other which quickly turned into rasslin' matches.

Back then I was 6'3" and weighed about 190 pounds. The new apprentice, Mark, had about 50 pounds on me plus he was a football player in high school. We were in the break room watching Price is Right one morning when he charged me like an offensive lineman and drilled me through the wall. I was unhurt, but we now had a 1 ½ foot by 2 foot hole in the break room wall. We panicked until clearer heads surfaced. Our initial action was to grab a Parker Funeral Home calendar, the old- fashioned giant one that had the planting times, phases of the moon and plenty of large date squares to record doctor appts.

We hung it over the hole, and it beautifully covered the collateral damage until we could find a better way to avoid detection. Tom even came in the room to raid the Hav-A-Snak box and was none the wiser.

The Hav-A-Snak box was placed on the break room table by a vender. It was on the honor system. It held Snickers, Milky Ways, Nutty Buddys, small bags of peanuts, chips, little packs of donuts and other delights that were heavy on carbs and calories but light on nutrition. You would take a snack and deposit a quarter in the attached box. Well, that was the theory. In practice most of the time, the poor box was violated. Repeatedly. Craig even pulled a mimed gun on the box and said, "Don't be a hero. Give up the M & M's!"

When the guy came to remove the box and vowed never to return because of "shortages," Don was livid. "That guy hant hount. Huts wrong with him?" I think myself, Tom, Don and Dennis were the only paying customers.

Back to the hole in the wall - in a group effort, we patched the wall with some scrap sheetrock and bought some paint that matched if you dimmed the lights. We decided to leave the calendar there and vowed to conduct our horseplay in the larger arena of the visitation common area between the layout rooms.

It was the best of times. It was the worst of times. I just had to add that in as I always thought if I ever wrote a novel, I would include something Dickensian. Let's go on a death call now. Come along for the ride. You may learn something.

Is She Dead?

Coldest night of the year so far. A couple of inches of snow on the ground. Still coming down and more forecasted. You don't get to pick and choose your nights on call. Into the deep realm of sleep where you incorporate the ringing of the telephone into your dream. Well, at least this was a house call. I wouldn't have to get out into this unfit night by myself. We always send 2 people on a residential call.

Dennis and I met at the funeral home and jumped into the hearse. This call was out in the county over some pretty rough roads. The bouncing of the hearse on the uneven pavement finally jarred me fully awake. We arrived at the farmhouse about 2:30 in the morning. We pulled the cot out of the back end of the hearse and maneuvered it through the snow up to the porch.

We rang the doorbell, and a sad and tired-looking lady greeted us. "I have been sitting up with Mom every night for the past week." I found this very noble and gently asked where Mom is right now. "She is in the back bedroom. Uh. Could you tell me if she is dead for sure?" WOW. My first thought was that she had very well better be dead to summon Dennis and me out in the middle of nowhere at this inconvenient and hideous time of the early morning. My next thoughts, which I discreetly kept to myself, were: I'm sorry but I left all my death detection tools back at the ranch. If you have a lighter, I can warm up a toe and see if she flinches. Or if you have a mirror, I can hold it to her mouth and see if it fogs up. I gently felt for a pulse and finding none, I pronounced her fit for a trip to the funeral parlor.

The scene of a death is always an intimate and reverent place to be. You cannot be trained on how to act or what to say. You must have sympathy and empathy and above all treat that

vacant earthly temple as if it were your own flesh and blood.
You cannot recoil in horror at the sight of blood or poop or
maggots. You must carefully put any sense of nausea or distaste
out of your mind and above all protect the head of the deceased.
Now is not the time for a misplaced step or cot malfunction. You
must simply do what is necessary because that is what YOU do,
and it IS necessary. I have often heard people complain about
undertakers and what a rip off they are and how they take
advantage of people. However "they" are the first folks people
call at 1 in the morning when they have had an unexpected death
and need the services and guidance of such a professional.

Just like a plumber, a doctor, or auto mechanic when you need
one, you NEED one. Once the leak is fixed or the appendix is out
or the transmission is fixed or the body is in the ground, the
thoughts of paying the bill become odiferous because there is
really nothing tangible to show for the services rendered.

I never understood why we were required to don a suit and tie
for death calls. Sure, they look professional when worn properly
(i.e. shirt tucked in, tie falling near the belt buckle, manufacturer
and price tag removed, cleaned every month or two), but when
the average director has 40 inches of belly hanging over 36
inches of pants, a tie tied to where it falls somewhere between his
2nd or 3rd button stained with yesterday or last week's
breakfast, the GQ tends to turn into EWW! Suits tend to soil
easily, especially at accident scenes or when the death occurred
long enough ago to liquify the remaining remains.

One afternoon someone found the body of a man who had
taken his life with a handgun to the head. He was lying on his
face in the middle of August in a field and when turned over
revealed an army of maggots doing what they do so well. His
wife insisted on saying goodbye before his cremation, so the best
we could do was douse him with disinfectant and cover him with
a sheet. We left his left arm visible so she could view his
wedding ring and hold his hand one last time. All went as well as

could be expected until out of the corner of my eye, I could see what appeared to be a long grain of white rice creeping down his arm. By double teaming, we were able to distract the new widow and convinced her to leave before the maggot could make his presence known to her.

Phone Etiquette

At the funeral home downtown, the phone was usually answered by one of the owners. Each had their own unique way of answering the phone.When receiving calls at a funeral home, you have to balance sympathy with sincerity and be diligent to put on your best vocal "face" every time you answer because you never know if it is a hospice nurse, a grieving spouse, a mother who has just lost her baby or on the other end of the spectrum an office supply company that wants to know if your copier is adequately handling your printing needs.

Charlie would always answer in a smooth and soothing southern drawl, "Good afternoon -- Parker's." Tom, on the other hand, would just pick up the receiver and say something that sounded like "Perkys." Then, Virginia was so sweet and apologetic and like a Jeopardy contestant would always answer the phone in the form of a question. "Parkers?" Don, the senior embalmer, didn't let his speech impediment deter him from answering the phone.

One afternoon the phone rang a couple of times and Don grabbed it. "Hmarker Huneral Hervice. How can I hep hyou" Of course all we heard was his side of the conversation, but his face told the story. Don: "Huh?" His face turned red. "Hpardon?" He shrugged his shoulders. "Ham, listen Ham. I hcan't hunderstand you!" He held the receiver out and told us, "I hcan't hunderstand a hword she is hsayin!" He spied Greg and in desperation said, "Hraig! Hraig! Take this hphonecall. I hcan't make out a hword she is hsayin!!" Greg took the receiver from Don and took over the call. He quickly determined how many death certificates the lady was requesting and gently hung up. He later informed us that the lady on the phone had the exact same speech impediment as Don.

Uncle Wallace

I had been working at the funeral parlor for about three months. I received word that my Uncle Wallace had been admitted to the hospital with a heart attack. I had just seen him mowing his lawn the previous week. Dennis invited me for a cookout after work that day. "Hey, Don Lee. I'm cooking out tonight. Wanna come over?" "Sure! Can I bring anything?" Dennis thought about it and said, "How about the meat. Can you bring the meat? Oh and some charcoal. Gonna need charcoal. And maybe some chips. We might need more drinks as well."

About six o'clock that evening after I had made a run to the store, Dennis sat down to relax, and I joined him. The charcoal was just glowing nice and red, and the steaks were sitting on a plate like a murder suspect in an interogation room - about to be grilled. Dennis was on call that night, and the phone in his house rang loudly; he had a ringer rigged outside so he could hear it in the backyard. This was pre pagers, pre beepers, pre cell phones. If you were on call, you stayed home.

Dennis took the call and came back out. "Sorry. Death call. Gotta go." Just out of curiosity I asked him the name of the deceased. "Uh, Wallace Lee."
That really cooled off the Bar-B-Que. "Dennis, Wallace Lee is my uncle!" And that started a long tradition of Dennis taking care of my family. He would go on to embalm 3 more of my uncles, their wives, my grandfather, great grandmother, my father, my first wife, and most recently my mother. We shared a bond as the years progressed because he lost his first wife right after she bore him his son. After dealing with her loss for a couple years, he started reading the Bible and was baptized. He would go on to study the Bible with me and was instrumental in

my salvation. Most folks have a lawyer or a doctor or a plumber of choice. I have my embalmer. Dennis. I have known him for 41 years and would literally entrust any body to his superior skills.

Director in Disguise

Dennis had moved on to the competitor and was gracious enough to take me along for the ride. Memorial Funeral Home was to be my home for the next 15 years. It was where I obtained my funeral director license.

One day I brought in a pair of Groucho Marx nose and glasses. If you have never seen such a disguise or sight gag, it would be well worth your effort to Google an image of it. It allowed the wearer to change the appearance of his nose while sporting black eyeglass frames and a bushy, black mustache. That pair of glasses brought years of fun to our home.

Mark, an embalmer with a preference for Budweiser and big, noxious cigars, was first to try them. We placed a towel from the back room around his head and the Groucho glasses. To complete the illusion, he silently puffed a cigar, turning the darkened arrangement office blue with smoke. We explained to the latest "counselor," a fancy name for a cemetery plot salesman, that Sayeed Fayade, a wealthy Saudi oil baron, was wanting to buy a couple of individual mausoleums for himself and his wife. In 1980, those puppies sold for about $20,000 each. David, the counselor, could see the commission dollars line dancing through his head.

He nervously entered the room to find Mark the embalmer stoically puffing his stogie and looking every bit the millionaire Arab prince. To each question asked, Mark simply puffed the cigar and gazed hypnotically at David. Finally after not being able to communicate with "Sayeed,' the counselor gave up.

The next fellow to use the Groucho glasses was Dennis, and it almost got him into trouble. We had completed a funeral, and Dennis was driving the hearse back from the attached cemetery

to the funeral home to set up for the next funeral. He grabbed
the glasses and donned them as a joke. Imagine his surprise
when he met the family of the lady we had just buried. They
stared at him as we drove by. Hopefully, they thought it was just
another employee. We always threatened to use those glasses for
any complaints. Want the manager? Pardon me a second while I
put on the Groucho glasses.

Scat Flak Attack

One morning we received the call to pick up a lady from the
Meadowbrook Manor. Nursing homes change their names like
some folks change their underwear. Wait until they reach a
certain level of olfactural offensiveness and then make a change.
No matter how many times you rename a nursing home, by its
very nature it is going to smell uh, well, like a nursing home.

This particular time it was going by the mellow, warm and
fuzzy name of Meadowbrook Manor. Previous incarnations
included Autumn Court, the Oaks, the Terrace and Leisure
Lodge. Nursing home calls were handled by one undertaker
because the decedent was usually in an adjustable bed, and there
was always a nursing assistant or custodian available to help
with the lifting - unless the body was unusually large. In that
case, I would simply reach all the way under the chuck, or
disposable pad, and pick them up gently and lay them upon the
cot.

Back in the 70's and early 80's, universal precautions were
unheard of. I never wore any gloves back then. On this
particular call, there seemed to be a slight problem. Flying feces.
You heard me right. I did say flying feces. Had there been a fan
in the room, I am sure it might have struck it as well. You see, it
was a double occupancy room, and they had left the decedent's
roommate on the portable potty too long, and she was reaching
under herself and flinging poop at anyone and everything. I
have observed primates in the St. Louis Zoo exhibit the same

behavior. What would Marlin Perkins do? He would get his trusty sidekick Jim to handle it, and then cue the Mutual of Omaha commercial. We could have waited until the poor pooper ran out of ammo, but there was always the threat that she might reload. I recruited a nurse's aide, and we decided to just make a frontal attack and swarm.

We procured a sheet from another room and prepared to catch a full-on frontal fecal flak attack. I grabbed one end of the sheet and the aide grabbed the other. Swarm! Swarm! Swarm! We held the sheet in front of us as a shield of armor and took her down. We neutralized the threat. She was given something to calm her down and moved from the room so I could remove her roommate. That was literally the first time I had ever literally taken crap from anyone. Just a little advice for future employees of Shady Acres or Wings of Compassion or whatever name the nursing home is going by now, get 'em off the pot in a timely manner or risk wearing human scat. That was the first and hopefully the last time I will ever have to face incoming human waste.

Death Makeover

I was dressing a lady one afternoon. Yes, I did say dressing her. You really didn't think they just put on their Sunday best and climbed into that casket with freshly-fluffed hair, did you? And yes, the undertaker does indeed make "alterations." Folks will bring in the suit that Dad wore to his wedding to his second wife 15 years ago and not even think about the fact that Dad had gained 68 pounds since then. Or maybe he suffered a lingering death from cancer and lost 68 pounds. That suit is not going to fit. Or will it? It will. Pants too tight? Cut the waistband in back. Jacket too small? Cut it all the way in half and button it back in front. Dress too small? Yup. Cut it up the back and lay it on Mrs. Jones and carefully tuck it around like a tablecloth.

We always keep a supply of new underwear - both men and women's. I am the champion and advocate for the dead. No one is going commando on my watch unless the family specifically calls for that.

Anyway, back to the story. I dressed the lady, put on her jewelry and grabbed her glasses off the counter. I sprayed Windex on them and gave the lens a good polish. I don't like dirty glasses, and I'm sure no one wants to rest for eternity with smudges on their lenses. We put her in the casket and wheeled it into the creaky old service elevator. At least this one had a motor. The one at the former parlor was operated by a rope and pulley system. Very archaic and old school.

I wheeled the casket into the visitation room and waited for Mr. Smith to view his wife for the first time since he had entrusted her into our care.

First viewings are emotionally charged and can be like walking through a minefield. You want to have EVERYTHING just right because any little thing can and will turn into a big thing simply because death renders us helpless, and the only one we can take our frustrations out at the time is standing right there within arm's reach. Too much make up. Not enough make up. The tie is crooked. That doesn't look a thing like Mom. His hair is parted the wrong way. Couldn't you make him smile? I was mentally going through everything that could go wrong when Mr. Smith turned to me and said those chilling words, "Don? She NEVER wore glasses." I was stunned and embarrassed and sweating and thinking of how many ways this was going to play out. I started with, "Well, Mr. Smith, I apologize! I am so sorry about this and we ..." "But Don? They really do look good on her. May we keep them on her?" Knowing that they were probably a pair that should have made it into the Lions Club donation box, I assured him that Yes! She may keep them.

Webekah Weaf

I was on my second cup of coffee and had just about finished the joke section of the "Dead Beat," a trade publication for and about funeral homes. I looked up in time to see an angry woman clutching the weathered remains of the "Rebekah Wreath."

The Rebekah Wreath is a large styrofoam R mounted on a metal easel that we put out at each funeral for a deceased member of the Rebekahs, the female service organization that is the counterpart to the Odd Fellows.

"WELL!! You wuined it!" This started her Elmer Fudd-fueled fiery compwaint."Pardon Me?" Yup that was all I had. A weak "Pardon Me?" "The Webekah Weaf. You wuined it!!" "I am sorry, Ma'am. How did.." And then came the priceless verbal assault that I can recite from memory word for word even though it happened at least 25 years ago. "You weft the Webekah Weaf out in the wain. It got all wusty."

Although I had no authority and was desperately trying to keep a straight face and civil tone, I asked her how we could make it right. "Well, maybe 25 dowwahs for matewials to make a new one. I need wots and wots of wibbon so I can we-wap the Awwah. And a new easow cause this one was weft out in the wain and is vewy vewy wusty." I left a sticky note for the manager so he could smooth the ruffled feathers. She received her $25, and a week or two later we had a shiny new "Webekah Weaf."

Jim

In my 40 years of funeral service, of the hundreds of funerals I attended or conducted, it became a funeral fact. Nobody went to hell. Everybody was preached into heaven. Most times the family had a spiritual counselor, but in the occasional time when the deceased did not have a church affiliation, we were asked by the trusting family if we knew anyone who would preach the funeral. One of my favorites was Jim. Some folks called him James, but I knew him as Jim because that's what my daddy called him. He and Jim had been friends for decades.

Physically, Jim was stuck in the fifties. He always wore his hair in a flat top, and his glasses hadn't seen a remake since Buddy Holly popularized the black nylon frames. Jim was a pleasure to be around and was always smiling. He was popular and in demand - weddings, funerals - you name it. He preached weddings and funerals for multiple generations of the same families. I don't even think Jim could tell you how many families he had served.

We were fortunate to get him to work some visitations for us, and it seemed everyone entering the funeral home knew Jim. One evening a lady entered the front door and spied Jim. "Well, hello, Brother Rogers. So good to see you. How are you doing?" Jim gave her a warm greeting and added, "Say,Helen. How is your mother getting along these days?" Her answer tickled me and embarrassed Jim. "Well, Brother Rogers, you preached her funeral about a year ago." Oops! Awkward!! Did it faze Jim? Not at all. His unflappability would come in very handy just a few weeks later.

An old boy named Larry died and his family could not afford a funeral. His lack of funds hampered his ability to pay for a decent burial until his brother cashed in his own funeral plan to pay for Larry's send off. Jim preached the funeral, and all went well until we pulled into the gates of the remote country cemetery. "That man looks angry." Jim verbalized what I was thinking. A few folks, obviously upset, were standing around the grave; when we exited the hearse, the "angry man" came charging at the hearse and lit into us with a verbal assault.

"Where's the (blankin') vault? You ain't gonna bury my daddy like a (blankin') dog without a (expletive deleted) vault." I calmly explained that the old country cemetery didn't require an outer container and that Larry's brother had paid for the funeral with his own funeral plan. "That worthless chicken (poop) uncle of mine didn't pay for a vault? Well, you ain't buryin' my daddy without one!"

In those days, we didn't have cell phones. The ungrateful son insisted that Jim stay at the cemetery with Larry and the hearse. He took me hostage, and we drove in his pickup to the nearest house where I used their landline to call the funeral home to have them order a vault. The indignant "indigent" son magically produced a credit card, and three hours later Larry was laid to rest in a vault.

The squeaky wheel gets the grease. The guys in the suits and ties get cussed. Jim preached my daddy's funeral in 1992 and would go on to preach many many more. The takeaway? Undertakers have to develop a thick hide yet maintain a tender side.

Chet

"Chet." Well, what has he done now? You ain't gonna believe what he pulled today. Memorial had an opening for an embalmer/funeral director and hired "Chet," a corn-fed, country boy from the Missouri-Iowa line, to fill the spot. Chet not only filled it but kept us entertained for the next 5 years as well.

Chet could greet a grieving family and take them crying into the arrangement office. Two hours later, they would emerge in a much lighter mood, hugging Chet and even offering him a chance to hunt on their land. The secret to Chet's charisma and also his talent for walking the tightrope between respect and ill-bred, downright uncouth actions was the fact that he was missing that part of the brain that filters thoughts BEFORE they are expressed verbally and physically. My dad had diagnosed me with the same affliction numerous times. He said I had a "serious couth deficiency."

I was serving in the capacity of Chet's obituary typist in the days before word processors - when one error could send you back to the typewriter again and again. He was gathering information from Mrs. Phelps, a respected Columbia business owner. Her husband had died rather suddenly, and she was giving Chet the details of exactly how she wanted his funeral to be staged. The door to the arrangement office was slightly ajar, and I could hear the following conversation as it played out.

Chet had a pleasant but acute regional country boy accent that endeared him to most folks but could be a turn off to the wrong person. I knew Mrs. Phelps could afford the best and heard Chad doing his best to sell the best. "Wahl, Mrs. Phelps, this here copper casket here is guaranteed. Yes, guaranteed. You could submerge it in a farm pond and it'd never leak. Never leak." Farm pond? Images of catfish bait entered my thoughts. Where in the world did that come from?

Later on in the arrangement, Chet inquired about the service details. "Wahl, Missus Phelps. Is there any song you want played at the funeral service?"
Mrs. Phelps: "Yes, Sir. I would like "Deep River" sung at the service." Chad: "Uh. Hmmm. Uh yes. Uh wahl. Deep Water. Nope, never heard of it." Mrs. Phelps: "No. I said, "Deep River." You know. "Deep
River." Chad: "Uh. Hmmm. Nope. Never heard of Deep River." Mrs. Phelps: "You know, it's an old negro spiritual Deep River." And then she proceeded to sing a line in one of those high-falutin' soprano voices. "Deep River, my home is over Jordan…" And then Chet being Chet uttered these words to the grieving widow: "Wahl, Missus Phelps. You know it so well, we'll just lat you sing it!" I couldn't see Mrs. Phelps face, but I know that my jaw dropped.

Another example of Chet's actions bypassing his brain occurred in the small bedroom community of Ashland, about 15 miles south of Columbia. Memorial bought the local funeral home there and established Chet as the local contact. He moved there, and in short order endeared himself to much of the town. We were in the hearse leading a funeral procession of about 10 cars right down the main drag.

Chet was driving and I noticed him giving friendly waves to folks he knew as we drove slowly down Broadway on the way to Highway 63 that would lead us to New Salem Cemetery. I elbowed Chet and said, "Hey! This ain't no parade. You can't be waving to everyone like this is the Funeral Home float." Without missing a beat or even thinking about consequences, Chet reached into his suit coat pocket as he hit the electric window down button in the hearse. "Ah yes. A parade. Um Hmm!" He then tossed a couple of Tootsie Rolls into the street. I was too embarrassed to see if any children darted out to collect the candy.

Chet was sitting in the front lobby one morning reading the newspaper. A gentleman he and I both knew walked in for his 10 AM arrangement conference. I got up and shook his hand, but Chet stayed seated. "Say Roy. Uh sorry about your mother. Yeah so sorry." Chet said this as he glanced over his newspaper. Roy just looked at Chet. Chet tried again, "Uh, sorry, Roy. Sorry about your father. " Roy finally glared at Chet and angrily spat out, "It's my wife!! My wife died!!" Chet was still seated and buried himself deeper in the newspaper and said meekly, "Uh sorry."

Chet became so popular in spite of (or because of) his loose cannon style that when he was fired a couple of years later, he got the backing of the town and was able to procure the financing to open his own funeral home that effectively closed the local funeral home down in short order.

The Ramseys

"Hey, Mama... Have you signed the register book yet?" I was pushing a gentleman into the chapel when I heard the all too

familiar voice of Mr. Ramsey coaxing his wife to sign the guest
book of a man whom I was certain that they had never known in
life. I never figured out if the Ramseys were funeral groupies or
simply had donated their brains to science before they were done
with them. They had deviled me during my tenure at Parkers
and had apparently found someone to give them a ride to
Memorial.

The Ramseys were a middle-aged couple whose only purpose
and joy in life was to attend funerals. They were always smiling,
grinning actually, just like they had good sense. They were very
pleasant as well as quite annoying. They always made a point of
signing the guest book before inquiring if the family was there
yet. If they timed their arrival just right, they would not only
greet the family but try to sit with them in the family room.
Their greatest joy seemed to be finding a family willing to let
them hitch a ride to the cemetery so they could extend their
adventure. You know, get a little more bang for the family's
buck.

One afternoon at Parkers, they tried the patience of the wrong
director, and the following debacle ensued. We were just about
ready to lock up for the day when the Ramseys appeared out of
nowhere. "Hey, Mama...did you sign the book?" Ma Ramsey
signed the register, and they headed into the chapel. They slowly
made their way to the front and approached the casket. We
could hear them mumbling up there, and finally Pa Ramsey left
Ma Ramsey and sought the help of Don, an embalmer who could
be rude for no reason on a good day.

"Sir? Sir? Hey! " Don asked them with all the fake sincerity
he could muster if there was a problem. "Me and mama can't
see the corpse." Don was puzzled. "Hlet me hadjust the mlights,"
he uttered. Don turned up the lighting. "I still can't see him,
Mama. Can you?" Pa Ramsey asked. Don was getting antsy. We
closed at 5, and he wanted to be home, beer in hand, and feet up
by 5:10. The casket was centered between 2 torchiere lamps. A

torchiere lamp is a tall floor lamp with a fluted decorative top that contains cosmetic lighting that can soften harshness, create a mood, and even hide subtle flaws on a restored body. These lamps usually stand about 5 feet tall.

Don grabbed the torchiere lamp at the head of the casket and thrust it in the face of the corpse like a hunter sighting in on a target. The torchiere lamp, suddenly six inches from the dead man's face, couldn't help but illuminate his visage to viewable levels. "Hcan you see him hnow? "HCAN YOU SEE HIM HNOWWW?"

The Ramseys left, and Don made it home for that first beer on time that day. The Ramseys also enjoyed hitching rides to cemeteries and wouldn't mind at all asking the widow or widower himself for a lift. I am sure that is how they wound up at Memorial Funeral Home as it had a large cemetery attached to it.

Funeral Home Fright

Weekends at the funeral home could either be nonstop activity, because weekends are the most popular time for funerals, or they could be long days spent cleaning, reading or watching cars pass by on Old Highway 40.

Some entertainment could be found watching the bar across the street, Chub's Club. I watched one day as two men staggered out of there arguing loudly and sizing each other up. The argument progressed to punches. Most punches missed their targets, but finally one man wound up his arm like Popeye the Sailor Man. I watched in awe as the other man in his drunken haze seemed mesmerized by this action. Popeye unwound a right uppercut that tapped the guy on the jaw, and the fight ended with a knockout.

Later that day, I was looking out the back window at the construction going on with the new addition. I noticed a kid on his bicycle. He looked to be about 8 years old. I decided to liven up his day and mine with a little harmless fun. His back was to me, and I was on the second floor. I silently opened the window and let out a banshee scream that echoed through the empty funeral home and scared the Skittles out of that little boy. I ducked and peeped out. He was looking around cautiously when I let him have it again, only louder.

This time he took off like a cartoon character pedaling furiously and not looking back. Ha! That was rich!! I was still chuckling to myself an hour later when the doorbell to the funeral home rang.

We locked the doors at noon on Saturdays if nothing was going on. I figured someone was probably looking for a grave location, so I took my time getting to the door. Imagine my surprise and horror as I opened the door to that young boy... clutching the hand of a policeman!! Rut Roh! I gulped and put my best funeral director face on.

"Hello, Officer! How may I help you?" "Well, sir. This young fellow here says that he heard cries for help coming from the funeral home." So the little rascal called the Po Po on me. I locked eyes with the policeman and told the truth. "I am the only one here at the funeral home. You guys are welcome to come in and look around." The kid sheepishly followed the cop into the funeral home, still keeping a death grip on his hand. We took a little tour, and as they left, the policeman gave me a knowing look and mentioned something about the kid's imagination.

When I told Dennis the story, he said I should have pulled my necktie into a noose and yanked my neck as the kid looked back at me. Somewhere there is a 45-year-old man who heard hideous screams coming out of a funeral home years ago. Sure hope it didn't mess him up too bad. I like to think that he went on to become a professional. Or a horror story novelist.

So kid, if you are reading this, yes, you really did hear hideous screams coming from the mortuary that fall Saturday afternoon long ago in Columbia, Missouri.

My dad always did say that you have nothing to fear from the dead. It's the living folks that you have to watch out for.

It Wasn't My Pleasure

In Columbia, one of our funeral assistants was also a local pastor whose weekly sermons were broadcast on the AM station KFRU. He was a likeable fellow whose voice was very warm and comforting. In fact, I had grown up listening to him and was amused when I actually met him because he sounded so much like himself.

"Richard" had one funeral sermon that was very much like a ball cap manufactured in China. One size fit all. I could sit outside the chapel and pretty much know what he was saying word for word. He did, however, throw in a touch of personalization. He would mention the name of the deceased at the very beginning. "It was not my pleasure to know Mrs. Jones, but in Paul's letter to the Corinthians, he mentions that God has prepared a house with many mansions..." Every once in awhile he would throw Mrs. Jones's name in the blank as he progressed to the inevitable and quite predictable conclusion.

One sunny afternoon he was preaching the funeral of Mr. Unterschutz. The embalmers and I were sitting outside the chapel halfway listening to the sermon. We always sat there waiting for the final prayer as that was our cue to enter the chapel, dismiss the mourners, and line up the pallbearers. Mike lit a cigar, and we were discussing yesterday's Mizzou Tiger football game. "It was not my pleasure to know Mr. Undershorts, but the Apostle Paul in his letter to.."

Mike was the one who caught it. "Did he say Mr. Undershorts??" Granted Unterschutz and Undershorts could sound the same ... kinda ... sort of ...well maybe.However, it was confirmed minutes later when Richard again mentioned Mr. Undershorts. In his defense, his Norwegian/Minnesota accent might have played a part in this nomenclatural faux pas. The family never mentioned it - either out of kindness to Richard or because they weren't listening closely either.

Grieving families don't ask a whole lot. Well, sometimes they do. But generally they are just trying to survive the surreal, yet all too real, reality of saying goodbye to their treasured loved one forever. A minimal requirement is getting the name of the deceased right. They might forgive mispronounced names of extended relatives or towns, but the name of the guest of honor, the star of the show, must be correct.

One afternoon we had a graveside service for a lady named Sarah. The local Catholic church sent over Father "Clarence." He was probably in his mid sixties, but his hair was dyed a burnished red and when combed, which was rare, he slightly resembled Bozo the Clown. Clarence usually had a slight buzz on, so it was hard to tell if he was just flat drunk or perhaps slightly in his cups.

Graveside services are usually brief, and Catholic graveside services are basically read from a book and generally contain a remark from the Padre and a response from the crowd. Sarah's family sat hushed as Clarence maneuvered himself between the elevated casket and the seated guests. "We are here to celebrate the life of our dear friend SUSAN."

Susan? I looked down at my feet. He must have called Sarah "Susan" 8 times before the last "And now may You bear the soul of our dear, dear SUSAN swiftly on the wings of angels to her eternal home with You in Heaven. Lord, hear our prayer." Each time he cut loose with a "Susan," instead of a "Sarah," the family winced and I cringed. Good thing God doesn't rely on us to record the names that are in the Lamb's Book of Life.

Biker Funeral

Dennis and I were scheduled to conduct the graveside service for a biker in the peaceful confines of Old Union Cemetery.

After a short and troubled life, he had finally overdosed on a mixture of high-dose painkillers and cheap whiskey. We got to the cemetery and were starting to unload the hearse when the family showed up and informed us they had arranged to have the funeral moved from graveside to inside the ancient country church because of the sweltering heat and humidity. Dennis and I welcomed that last-minute change. We were thankful for the air conditioning until we realized we hadn't brought a church truck with us. A church truck is the silver or gold color device with wheels mounted on it that the casket rests upon. Undertakers have to improvise and roll with whatever comes along. We removed the flowers from the altar table and had the motley crew of pallbearers carry the casket all the way from the back of the hearse to the front of the church.

Biker funerals are casual affairs. In fact the best-dressed pallbearer was wearing a wife beater tank top T shirt and jogging sweatpants. Oh and cowboy boots! We pinned the boutonnieres or corsages on the bearers. I always found it awkward to attach a flower to another man; in this case, it was especially hard to pin a flower on the strap of a T shirt, but we got 'er done. Everyone settled in, and things were going pretty well right up until the preacher opened his mouth. "There is only one thing and one reason to blame for the fact that we are here today. Yes, friends, it is THAT DEMON ALCOHOL!!!" Dennis and I had heard this before and were prepared for the rest when a big, mean-looking guy with assorted tattoos, bulging biceps, and a ponytail hanging out of his doo rag jumped up and yelled, "I don't have to listen to this (crap)." And just like that we had lost our first pallbearer. Eventually by the end of the funeral, we still had 3 pallbearers left plus Dennis and myself to carry the fellow to his grave. Funerals are for the living, not the dead. Sometimes the living don't listen either.

The Most Wonderful Time of the Year

Christmas was always a festive time around the funeral home. My first exposure to a holiday in funeral land left a slight bitter taste in my mouth. At Parker's, the owners didn't think it fair to just let a few employees off, so they required everyone, owners included, to show up and sit there "waiting for the call." In my mind, I can picture a Norman Rockwell painting of all seven of us
(Don, Dennis, Craig, Tom, Charlie, Virginia and myself) entitled "Waiting for the Call," a cheerless portrait of seven folks thrown together at work on the holiday of holidays because the owners had no families of their own to speak of and wanted to treat the employees fairly by letting no one off. They did give us cash holiday bonuses and were very lenient in other ways, so I will always remember them fondly.

At Memorial the cash bonuses were always given by the manager, David, at the staff Christmas party. One year he sent Mike, the senior embalmer, to procure the cash for the bonus giveaway. David would give each employee $100 at the party. Mike came back with 10 one hundred dollar bills. On his way to David's office, he immediately flashed his wad of cash to the newbie embalmer. "Hey Gus. Look what David gave ME this year for a bonus!! Yup. One thousand dollars!"

Russ was overcome by jealous anger and immediately raced into David's office."Hey! Where's my thousand dollar bonus??" David ordered him out of his office.

At the Christmas party that year before the bonuses were handed out, David allowed me to sing the touching song I had written to the tune of that old Nat King Cole song "The Christmas Song." Maybe you know it as "Chestnuts Roasting on an Open Fire." Here is my song written especially for the party that year:

Oak box resting on a catafalque. Batesville coming everyday. Five car pileups and the outbreak of flu, Yes, death is surely here to stay. Everybody goes - no refunds no exchanges here. We

will put you in your place. And so if you're close to the edge of
your grave….
Buy a lawn crypt. Buy a lawn crypt. Buy a lawn crypt to——
day…"

I don't care when they planned the party, someone was always
guaranteed an early exit to pick up someone. I can't tell you how
many Christmas Eve dinners or Christmas morning gift
openings or Christmas Day dinners were interrupted by the
Grim Reaper.

One memorable Christmas Eve, Dennis's brother Dave and I
got the call to pick up an elderly lady at her residence. We
entered the house and found her lying on the kitchen floor where
she had fallen and was pronounced by law enforcement as DRT
Dead Right There. As I was wondering if she had choked to
death on a slice of turkey or simply succumbed to a massive
heart attack, I noticed Dave surreptitiously finishing a beautiful
dinner roll he had pilfered from the pan on the stove. I was too
amazed to dwell on his actions because I was dwelling on what
was going on in the adjacent dining room. Grandma must have
been a wonderful cook because the gathered family, about 15
folks by my estimate, were chowing down and cramming the
wonderful dinner down their pie holes with great gusto with
Grandma lying belly up just 12 feet away. All in all, it was a
stirring tribute to Grandma's talent in the kitchen. Mourn the
loss but pass the pecan pie.

Donuts, Anyone?
At Memorial, the protocol for being on call was that you were
allowed to take the removal van home with you the nights you
were on call. This cut down response time quite a bit. Early one
morning about 1:30 AM, I was roused from a deep sleep by the
ringing of the bag phone. The early incarnation of the cell phone
was a bag the size of a purse containing a battery the size of a
brick and the phone receiver. I was given the name and the

address of the death by the answering service and wondered why it sounded so familiar to me - 1604 Parklawn Court. Hmm. Orville Catron. Hmmm. Wait a minute. That's my next-door neighbor. Awkward!! I threw on my suit and walked out the front door. Didn't even have to move the van from my driveway. Dennis pulled up shortly. We pulled the removal cot from the back of the van, rolled it next door, knocked on the door, proceeded to the back bedroom and gently placed the old gentleman on it.

His family watched as we loaded him into the van in my driveway. It was one of the easiest house calls yet one of the most difficult calls I was to make.

Later that winter I made a routine hospital removal and was amazed at how well the van handled in the 8 inches of snow that powdered the city streets. I safely made it back to the funeral home and deposited the deceased into the cooler.The funeral home was adjacent to a large cemetery that looked even more peaceful and serene under the fresh blanket of snow. It was now 3 o'clock in the morning, and I was wide awake. Before leaving the cemetery for the warm confines of my home to try to catch another couple hours of sleep, I couldn't pass up the opportunity for a little fun. An empty removal van and a cemetery with 8 fresh inches of snow equals donut-cutting fun. I was gunning it, sliding, braking hard, swerving to the left and then to the right, slinging snow in the parking lot and just having a great time in the winter wonderland. About ready to call it a night, I glanced over at the Business Loop and saw a police patrol car slowing down. I decided to end my Winter Olympics and sneak out the back exit of the cemetery. I looked in the rearview mirror, and the police car had turned into the cemetery. I was slowly driving by the mausoleum when the cop car lit me up. Pretty blue and red lights were swirling, and I decided I had better stop.

The policeman approached my rolled-down window and asked me what I was doing in the cemetery at 3 in the morning cutting donuts in the snow. When you can't think of a good excuse, you tell the truth. I told him I worked for the funeral home and had just dropped one off and decided to have a little fun before heading home. I will never forget his kindness when he said, "Oh. O.K., Son. We do that too; only we call it practicing evasive maneuvers. Be careful and have a good evening." Gave me a warm and fuzzy on that bitter cold morning. I was released on my own recognizance and was able to grab that extra couple hours of sleep.

Street Walker

You run across some different experiences when you are out running the streets at a time when most decent people are in bed. It was about 2 AM one crisp, early autumn morning when I finished making a hospital removal and had deposited the deceased at the funeral home for his appointment with the embalmer later that morning. I was leaving the funeral home when I noticed the fuel gauge was close to empty. I knew I would not have enough gas if I got another call that night, so I headed to the closest Shell station. The funeral home had an account there, so I pulled in and started the pump.

As I filled the tank, I noticed a young lady standing outside the station on the sidewalk. Alone and vulnerable, she appeared nervous and looked like a mugging victim waiting to happen. I finished gassing up the van and then went inside and signed the ticket. As I exited the station, I caught her eye and innocently asked her if she needed a ride somewhere. I just didn't want her to be stranded there all night or maybe fall victim to someone that would harm her at that dangerous time of the night. She eagerly got in the passenger side, and we pulled out of the gas station onto West Boulevard. I asked her where I could take her. She softly said, "Is there anything I can do for YOU?" My marriage passed before my eyes as I slammed on the brakes. "Get out!" I said abruptly.

She again asked how SHE could help ME. I told her to get out or I would take her directly to the police station. She decided that I was serious and complied with my wishes. She hopped out, and I headed straight home.

I shuddered to think of the possible alternative outcomes of that encounter. She could have accused me of picking her up and then attempted rape or any other equally hideous scenario. All these years later, I still get a rise when I tell folks about the night I picked up a prostitute. A live prostitute at that.

Gently-Used Recliner

One evening about 8 PM, Dennis and I caught a residential call. Not a bad time for a call. The gentleman was in his recliner in the living room. So far, so good. The protocol for removing a body from a recliner is to roll up a sheet and slide it under the body. Once the sheet is underneath, you can easily pick the decedent up and deposit them on the cot. As we slid the sheet under the body, I immediately noticed a "problem." The sheet was going in the one side a whiter shade of pale. However, after passing under the body, it was turning a suspicious fecal tone of brown. Then the unmistakable smell of pure diarrhea wafted from the confines of the corduroy Lazyboy. OK. Not a problem. We're both grown men. Seen that. Smelled that. Been there. Done that.

We got the befouled body tucked into the sheet and secured him to the cot with seat belts. Yes, seat belts. We then placed the cot cover that looked like it was made from Elvis's bathrobe, a royal blue velvet cover with "MEMORIAL" stitched in white letters across it. I never did understand why we had to advertise on the corpse blanket, but it is a time- honored tradition.

We rolled the cot to the front door and were exiting the porch when I heard a ruckus behind us. Sounded like someone was dragging something across concrete. I glanced behind me and could barely contain my amusement. A couple of the family members were dragging the soiled recliner outside. We loaded the decedent into the van as the family dragged the poopy recliner to the curb. As we left the driveway, Dennis asked me what was so funny. All I could think about was when some poor college kid drove by and saw the fairly new recliner sitting on the curb. I could see him and his buddies loading it up for a trip to their dorm. I still get tickled by the thought of what happened when they got a real whiff of their new chair.

Wheelchair Dry Run

Most funeral homes and churches keep a wheelchair or two around just in case a patron needs help from the parking lot to the chapel and vice versa. The old wheelchair at Memorial looked like it had been in use since Truman was in the White House, and finally WD-40 and a pair of vice grips could no longer keep it in fighting shape. Before we suffered a serious malfunction or an "incident" leading to involvement of lawyers, the owner decided to just bite the bullet and shell out the bucks for a nice deluxe model with all the latest bells and whistles.

He even sprang for the "wide load" model as he could see America getting larger with each generation. The much-anticipated wheelchair arrived one slow day at Memorial. It was already mostly
assembled except for the footrests and head rest contraption. We eagerly finished putting it together. A coin toss decided which director would get the inaugural ride in the fancy new wheelchair. Chet won the toss, and I was given the honor of pushing him around the funeral home to test each door and make sure it would fit through every nook and cranny and bathroom door before the actual need arose. We wanted that thing in tiptop shape. Chet took a seat. He looked much like a decorated general reviewing his troops as I wheeled him into the chapel, out into the hallway and into the arrangement office.The

extra wide wheelchair even made it into the bathrooms effortlessly. In fact, everything went well until it didn't.

The front entrance of the building had a nice 25 foot ramp that sloped down to the parking lot. I wheeled Chet toward the glass front door, and Mike the embalmer held it open like a gentleman. At the last second, I decided to REALLY test the new chair. I gave Chet a final push, well actually a pretty good shove, and sent him careening down the ramp. His flapping tie and blowing hair complimented his wild yell as the ride came to its inevitable conclusion at the bottom of the ramp. The wheelchair hit a parking block and stopped abruptly. Chet pitched out of the chair onto the asphalt surface of the parking lot. The wheelchair was on its side, one wheel still spinning, and Chet was sitting on the ground beside it. The chair passed the test and was no worse for the wear. Chet was mostly unscathed except for a bruise or two. Mike and I were laughing so hard we didn't even stop to think how that stunt must have looked to anyone driving down the Business Loop. Fortunately, this was decades before everyone had a video recorder on their phone. Slow day plus new wheelchair equaled precious memories.

What Time Is It

Nursing home calls were pretty routine. Usually, a nurse would send a CNA to lead the way to the room of the deceased and offer help if needed. During the wee hours of the night/morning, the nursing homes were pretty well understaffed, so I tried not to be too needy on these calls. I caught the call to head over to Candlelight Lodge early one morning.

Candlelight Lodge had been built in the 40's, and it had narrow hallways and small rooms. It was a neat, old building if you weren't incarcerated there. I checked in at the desk and was given the room number. I let the lady know I would come get her if I needed any assistance. I found the room, and the cot was just barely able to fit through the door. The recently departed was resting on his back on top of the covers like he was just stretched out for a nap. I quickly judged him to be well within my "lift limits."

Anybody at bed level, below 150 pounds I could simply reach under and literally pick them up and gently place on the cot. Larger individuals required use of a plastic board to slide them over onto the cot. His room was dimly lit, and I was lost in my own thoughts as I picked him up from the bed. Right after we had lift off but before we had splash down, I was startled by a disembodied voice very close to my ear. The mechanical voice advised me, "It is 4 AM." Two things went through my mind. Why does this man care what time it is and why is he telling me?

I had never conversed with the dead and had always imagined a conversation deeper than the time. Maybe a discussion of the weather? How long since his kids had visited him? Did he want to be embalmed or cremated? Nope. A simple declaration of the time. I was glad the cot was so close or I feared I could have dropped him from fright.

A closer examination revealed that he had one of those watches for the visually impaired that announce the time audibly. This feature must have been triggered by movement. That was the first and thankfully the last time I talked to a corpse. Well, actually just listened.

A couple of weeks later we received a house call. The decedent was a typical, little, old lady that had died in an upstairs bedroom. We always left the cot in the van until we established where in the house the body was and if we would need the foldable

stretcher for more inaccessible places. If the deceased was very large, our only option was to place them in the thick, zippered, black body bag and gently slide them down the stairs. We scoped out this particular removal, and I determined that we could not fit a cot or stretcher around the tight turn in the stairwell. I had Dennis stand by the cot at the bottom of the stairs while I picked up the little, old gal in my arms. She couldn't have weighed 75 pounds nightgown and all.

I was halfway down the stairs when the lights went out in the stairwell. There I was halfway down the stairs with a dead lady in my arms and couldn't see the next step. I stopped and waited until Dennis flipped the lightswitch back on. I had bumped it off with my elbow on the way down. With the pathway illuminated once again, we successfully transferred her onto the cot and went on our way.

Cremation Trials

Back in 1978, when I started my journey into the mysterious world of all things funeral, cremation was a rare option that usually only highly-educated folks resorted to. In the 70's, there were only a handful of crematories in the state of Missouri. If you wanted that option back then, it involved a two-hour trip either to Kansas City or St. Louis.

By the late 80's, Parkers had installed a retort (cremation oven), and the owner at Memorial saw the writing on the wall. By 1992, Memorial had a retort as well. Getting a crematory up and running involves a myriad of permits and zoning and headache-inducing paperwork. Not to mention the $100,000 for the building and another $75,000 for the retort itself.

By April, we had everything ready to go except for the fact that before you are granted the license, you must conduct a stack test to make sure the emissions are within government standards. Simply put, you needed a willing volunteer to be the first to climb in. Because cremation was still fairly rare, we did not have a client yet to try out the new oven.

After waiting a couple of weeks, we decided to test the retort by using a hog. Hogs are approximately the weight, and sadly, the build of a lot of folks. A good-sized hog was acquired and was loaded into the back of "Brian's" (another embalmer) new-to-him Chevy pickup. Brian and Dennis drove to the back of the

40 acre cemetery to put the hog down with a 22 bullet to the head. Just as Brian was going to deliver the kill shot, an elderly lady came driving around the corner presumably to put some flowers on a grave. This spooked both Brian and the hog. The first shot missed the hog but blew out his back window glass taking the rearview mirror out as well.

The lady wisely drove on, oblivious to the unfolding pathos, and the execution was back on track. Nothing to see here, folks. Go back to your homes. No last minute reprieves. They drove the remains to the crematory, a nondescript building towards the back of the cemetery. It looked like a detached garage. The only giveaway to its function was the 3 feet of smokestack running out of the top of the building.The sacrificial hog was loaded into the retort. There would be no pork steaks, pork chops,pork ribs, pork roast, McRib, pork butt, pulled pork, bacon or sausage. Two hours at 1600 degrees left only a few bone fragments. The crematory was pronounced in compliance with all emission testing, and we were ready for a more conventional use of the retort.

We were all given at least 10 or 15 minutes training on how to operate the new device. Word spread quickly about our new crematory, and soon we were going from one a week to one or two a day.

I was so excited my first time that I totally forgot about the cool-down time between cremations. After the cremation, you must wait an hour or two for the oven to cool down before placing the next body in. I raked out the still-glowing bone fragments into the steel pan and set it aside to cool enough so I could run the magnet through them to make sure no metal remained that would damage the processor. Staples from the cremation container, screws, pins and other debris from orthopedic surgeries all had to be removed. The bone chunks then "processed" into a consistency suitable for the urn or scattering.

I totally forgot about the cool down and started rolling the next body in while the oven was still at about 850 degrees.They say you ain't doing it right if you don't burn the hair off your arms. Just a joke, all you OSHA fans. I knew I was in trouble as the cremation container caught fire immediately as I was rolling it in. I put the door down and hit the start button. Not only did we have lift off, we had flames shooting out the top of the stack along with black smoke. In a panic, I called the funeral home. "Dennis! There's flames and smoke coming out of the crematory stack. What do I do?" Dennis calmly told me to shut off the retort, and hopefully things would work out. That did the trick. I was relieved that no one witnessed the flames shooting out. I was certainly not looking forward to a visit from the Fire Department or the Environmental Protection Agency. I am sure the emissions exceeded the governmental limits that day.

Later that month, a gentleman called the funeral home one day to inquire about the cost of cremating his foot. He was diabetic and his disease had progressed to the point of amputation. He wanted that foot to be cremated so that when he died, they would have ALL of him. I resisted the urge to tell him that it would "cost him an arm and a leg just to cremate a foot."

Firing up the retort uses a lot of natural gas. Whether it is because of the cost being comparatively cheaper than ground burial, or the portability of the cremated remains, cremation has now become more popular than traditional burial. A popular question that gets asked about cremation is the legality of scattering the cremated remains. My thoughts and advice have always been to dispose of them reasonably. Downwind preferably. I have never heard of anyone being arrested or prosecuted for scattering cremated remains.

Another bit of advice that you didn't hear from me is to purchase your urn online. The urns in the showroom at your local funeral home are very nice and high quality. The urns being offered online are very nice and high quality as well. Only they are about 60 percent cheaper. Most all of funeral merchandise these days is made in China anyway.

My approach to the selling part of the funeral has always been to show all the options and then step out of the room and let the family discuss what they can and cannot afford. My goal was always to not add any stress to an already broken heart.

Traffic Stop

Winter was always a rough time to work at a funeral home. We didn't get "snow days" or time to wait for the roads to clear. People die at all times of the night or day regardless of the weather.

One day in mid January, I slowly made my way through the icy streets and slid into the parking lot of Memorial. The parking lot hadn't been sanded yet, so I was extra cautious as I walked sideways in a crouch so I wouldn't have as far to fall if I slipped. I was much younger then, and falls were more of a nuisance than a broken bone. I was on my second cup of coffee and congratulating myself for making it into work safely when the phone rang. Hoping for a wrong number or a simple question about already scheduled services, I gingerly picked up the receiver.

Well. That's not good - a pedestrian killed out on Highway HH. Realizing that I was the only one who had made it to work that morning, I was charged with the hideous task of getting back out on those icy streets to pick up the "coroner call." HH is a narrow, two-lane highway about 5 miles north of Columbia.

The highway was blocked off, but I was motioned by the police to go ahead and proceed to the bottom of a steep hill where the accident had occurred. I carefully exited the van and immediately saw a shoe on the icy pavement and noticed a body off in the frozen grass. The deputy coroner filled me in on the sad details of the demise. "He couldn't make it up the hill and slid off. He was out of his car at the BOTTOM of an ice-covered

highway trying to stop traffic. Trying to warn folks to turn around I guess. Some lady saw him and hit the brakes. Coasted downhill and plowed right into him."
I had always heard about someone being knocked out of their shoes but had never seen such. Until that icy morning.

Jo, the deputy coroner, helped me wrestle the rather large and freshly-deceased man onto the cot. I figured the extra weight in back of the van would give me more traction on the way back to the funeral home. I decided to continue on HH and take the longer, yet safer, way back to the main highway. I cautiously crept up the hill. So far so good. I figured if I maintained about 20 miles an hour, I would be OK. Wait a minute. Where did this sharp curve come from? The road curved to the right, but we (the dead man and I) didn't. Faster than you can say, "Oh crap!!" we were off in the ditch. It was surreal to be sitting at a 90 degree angle in an icy ditch with a dead man for company. Poor fellow. His second accident happened within a couple miles of his first.

Now, this was a decade before cell phones. I was able to open the driver side door and crawl out. I had to skate across the icy pavement but had really caught a break. A house was only about 200 feet away. I knocked on the door and told my sad tale to the wide-eyed occupant. She gave me some coffee and allowed me to call the funeral home.

They called a tow truck, and because of the weather and numerous other wrecks, I had to wait another hour for the tow. It was about noon when I triumphantly backed into the unloading bay at Memorial. I learned a couple of valuable lessons that day: Don't try to stop traffic at the bottom of an icy hill, and an extra 250 pounds of weight in the back of a vehicle doesn't improve traction on ice. I would later go on to hit a pedestrian my own self on another icy road. That happened on my own time and is another story all on its own. O.K. if you insist I will tell you all about it...in the next chapter.

You Killed Him

"You killed him!" Does that statement grab your attention? It sure grabbed mine. Picture a

Saturday night in early December. December 7. A night that would live in infamy. My wife Robbie and I decided that we wanted to get out of the house. Maybe make a grocery run. Get some snacks before the next wave of weather hit. The light rain wasn't going to stop us. We headed out and stopped at our church building since it was around the corner, and I was curious to see who was scheduled to preach in the morning.

On the way back to our Escape, I noticed a little ice starting to form on the metal railing. Should we go back home or finish our snack run? We proceeded to the grocery store and collected our snacks. I pulled out onto the outer road, and we were discussing the viewing options for the evening. "I don't know if there is anything good on tonight."

"Maybe we should have rented a movie." I was starting to answer Robbie when the Escape started sliding. Unbeknown to us, we had hit a patch of black ice. The Escape did a 360 and then started propelling itself into the other lane. We saw oncoming headlights in the distance. Those few seconds seemed to last for hours. We had dodged the oncoming traffic when I saw the figure walking in the road directly in the path of our out-of-control Escape. Robbie yelled out in a panic, "You're going to hit him!" And we did. Like a bowler picking up a spare, our Escape had turned completely around, struck the pedestrian, and then slid back end down the embankment.

Robbie's first words of encouragement were, "You killed him?!?" I told her to call 911 as I jumped out of the SUV. I saw the dazed pedestrian. She was lying on her back and moaning. I then asked the stupid question that my panicked brain insisted I must ask. I leaned down and fearfully asked her, "Are you O.K.?" By then another car had stopped, and the kind gentleman noticed that we were all in shock. He encouraged me not to render any kind of assistance until the paramedics arrived.

I heard sirens, and they were there within 5 minutes.The policeman did not issue me any ticket as I was not impaired or careless. He admitted they had talked to her before about walking on a shoulderless highway. Robbie and I were like zombies. After the pedestrian was loaded into the ambulance, a tow truck pulled us out of the ditch. It looked like we had hit a deer.

We were sickened by the busted windshield and busted headlight and dented fender - not because of the damage. That was fixable. We were worried that the poor lady was going to die or suffer lifelong injuries.

Certain that our lives were ruined and that I had probably killed her, we didn't sleep much at all that night. I was still shook up and missed work the following Monday. I was devastated. I couldn't bear to think I had killed her. We were advised by our insurance company not to contact her due to possible legal action. To make this long story short, the bottom line is that she wound up in the hospital for a couple of weeks with a broken pelvis. She settled with the insurance company. I thank God I didn't kill her. I will never ever forget the nauseating and dreadful feelings surrounding the entire incident. Your life can change in a heartbeat. Always thank God for His goodness and care. Pray for His protection. Talk to Him daily. Don't just call Him when you need something.

Dental Accoutrements

A young politician on the rise from Columbia known for how fast she could get from Columbia to St. Louis, a distance of 125 miles, took I-70 a little too fast that crisp autumn morning and flew off the highway. Her small sports car overturned several times before coming to rest on its top. What a terrible tragedy and waste to have her life cut short just when she was at the start of a brilliant career! She was only 34 years old and so full of unfulfilled promise. Her family wanted her to have a full funeral with the body present and cremation following. The death certificate had to be signed before cremation could take place, so we were on a pretty tight schedule to make that happen. The coroner of the county where the death occurred was a dentist as well as coroner. Back then, the coroner was an elected official who needed no medical experience or training. Usually, the local undertaker doubled as the coroner.

Our people contacted his people, and we determined a date and time when he would be in his office. "Chet" was chosen to make the hour-long journey over to the county seat and track down the dentist. He was gone two or three hours; just when we were starting to get worried about him, he pulled into the parking lot. Chet leisurely strolled into the funeral home and sat down in the office. "Hey, Chet. Did you get the death certificate signed?" We anxiously asked. He appeared deep in thought and reached into his suit coat pocket. "Wahl, lookie here, fellows. I got me a new toothbrush." He actually had grabbed a half dozen. "And some toothpaste." "Some toothpaste" meant he had grabbed another half dozen of the dental office giveaways. "You guys need any mouthwarsh?" Yes, his other pocket held a handful of mouthwash samples. "Chet! The death certificate! Did you get the death certificate signed??" Chet looked thoughtful and said, "Uh. He wasn't in the office today. I think we're gonna have to go back another time." No death certificate, but we did have enough travel samples of dental products to keep our teeth happy for a while.

Sales Pitch

During my 40 years in the death care industry, I saw sales counselors come and go. Sales counselor,funeral plan salesman, pre-need counselor, burial plan salesman, cemetery counselor.

These hardy souls worked only on commission and earned their meager fare by selling funeral plans and cemetery plots before the need on the installment plan. It was a pretty hard sell trying to peddle something that most folks didn't want to think about anyway. When you have a house payment and a car payment, the last thing and I mean literally the LAST thing you want to spend your hard earned money on is something you won't get to enjoy any way until after you die.

I saw many people come and go trying to make a living in funeral sales. The one exception to this was an Arkansas fireball out of Pine Bluff named Veronica. Her perfectly-coiffed red hair probably hasn't been natural for at least 20 years. She was always impeccably dressed in a suit and used her southern drawl to great advantage. One of her favorite tricks was to grab the register book after the funeral started and copy the pages of names to gain her some leads of prospective victims.

We had just started a funeral for a gentleman that was a member of the Fraternal Order of the Elks. She grabbed the guest book and started walking toward the office copier; she waved the book gleefully at me and declared confidently, "It's Elk season, Honey! It's Elk season."

She would do anything to close a sale. One day she brought in a contract along with a dozen credit cards. I asked her why so many cards."Well, Honey, he wants $25 on the Visa card, $15 on the American Express, $30 on the MasterCard, $50 on the CitiBank card......" After we ran all the cards, she had enough for the $200 down payment which magically amounted to her commission on that deal. Who cares if they couldn't make another payment? At least she got her cut.

I asked her the key to her success, and she looked me straight in the eye and said, "Well, Honey,you got to learn to lie with integrity!" Wow! We often accused her of taking a contract to a hospital room or hospice bedside, placing a pen in the hand of the nearly dead, placing the contract under the pen, and then shaking the bed to move the pen for a semblance of a signature.

She was head of the sales department and one of her duties was to train the newbies, or "novice counselors," in the art of pre-selling death care and death care products. She took a young man named Maurice under her wing and gave him some of her advice. "Honey, when it comes time to close the deal, just tell them there are only 2 reasons why they wouldn't give this incredible gift of love to their family. Either not enough love. Or not enough money." I asked Maurice how that was working for him. "Well, Mr. Smith invited me into his living room and I showed him all the plans and options. He was kind of back pedaling and making excuses, so I said, 'Mr. Smith. There are only 2 reasons why you wouldn't give this gift of peace of mind and love to your family. Either not enough love or not enough money. Now, which is it, Mr. Smith?' " I said, "Oh yeah? What did he say?"

Maurice looked sheepish and said, "He threw my (behind) out of his house and told me to never come back." I didn't have the heart to tell him that Veronica could get away with this kind of behavior, but this kind of disrespect coming from a young pup would always get him thrown out.

My grandfather Noah Lee didn't suffer fools or peddlers. His sage advice to me that I will always remember is "Don't let anybody into your house that you ain't big enough to throw out!"

One last sales joke before we move on. Fred: I ain't buying my wife a birthday present this year. Zed: How come? Fred: She didn't use the present I got her last year. Zed: Well what was it? Fred: A cemetery plot.

Slap Stick Service

Flowers. Beautiful floral tributes. Gorgeous bouquets. Basket of Spring. Autumn Creations.

Peace Lilies. Ficus Trees. Waves of Poinsettias. Ask any funeral director that has to haul those things around, and he or she will call them what they are. Weeds!!

Let's just figure out how many times the average "floral tribute" is handled before it reaches its final destination either grave top or the family's living room. The tribute is purchased at the retail flower shop. Conservatively, we will say it costs 50 bucks. It is delivered to the funeral home where it waits, along with its floral brothers and sisters, for placement in the visitation room. A funeral director will place it nicely on display by the casket. Later as more flowers arrive, it is moved again. After visitation, the casket, along with all the flowers, are moved into the chapel. Or the whole shooting match is hauled to a church where everything is set up once again. After the funeral, it is hauled again. Cut flower arrangements will head on to the cemetery, and the potted plants and silk arrangements will be delivered to the family home. Some of the cut flowers will even make it to nursing homes. By the end of this cycle, the floral tributes are much worse for the wear.

An average funeral might net 15 arrangements, whereas a prominent death could attract as many as 50 or 60. We are talking thousands of dollars spent on flowers, most of which will be dead on the ground within 3 days. The average casket spray runs $250. OK. Rant over.

One of my top 10 funeral bloopers occurred at the Calvary Baptist Church in Columbia, MO. Dennis and I had gotten there very early so that we could set the memory picture perfectly. The deceased was popular enough to attract 8 stands of flowers that displayed 4 arrangements each. The funeral went off without a hitch, the eulogy was heartfelt, and the hymns played by the church organist were very inspirational. Due to the large crowd, we had four directors working that funeral. A couple of funeral directors were dismissing the crowd, and Dennis and I were packing flowers out to the flower van. Because of my height, I grabbed a couple of mixed arrangements from the top of the racks. Concentrating on getting a good hold on those arrangements, which depending on the florist and how much water was in the base, could weigh up to 25 pounds each, I promptly missed a step down and started a domino-effect fall. I had both arms full of floral tributes and crashed into a flower-laden rack. The momentum of my fall, combined with my more than generous proportions and larger-than-life girth, caused rack number 2 to take out rack number 3 which took out rack number 4. Counting the 2 in my arms, I single handedly managed to destroy about 18 flower arrangements with one Kramer-like misstep. Yes, I was thoroughly embarrassed, but like my 7-year-old daughter likes to say after a particularly dangerous-looking stunt, "I'm OK."

I heard snickering as I picked myself up. Who in the world would laugh at a funeral? I glanced over toward the right of the chapel, and the organist was openly belly laughing at my expense. In fact, most of the folks who hadn't made it out of the church were elbowing each other and pointing. I beat a hasty retreat and hid out in the flower van until what was left of them were loaded for their journey to the cemetery.

Did you ever try to clean flower pollen, flower juice and flower water out of a suit? The flowers won that day, but I would live to mishandle many more beautiful floral tributes.

Flips and Flops

Spills and leakages can wreak havoc on the flooring material of the removal van. Back in the old days, this was not a problem because we used the hearse, and its fancy decking was both beautiful and impervious to spilled bodily fluids. Face it. With the dead, you never know if blood, pee, poop, vomit, decomposition or the stray maggot (or two) will find its way out of the bag and embed itself in the carpet. I say all that to say this. We constructed a platform of plywood and used flooring tiles to cover it. This new deck was easy to clean yet very slick. We neglected to put recessed cups in the floor to hold the cot legs in place. Not a problem until it was. Of course, the problem manifested itself on my watch.

I had made a routine removal from the hospital. I was executing a right turn when the cot slid and flipped to the right. Having no knowledge of physics but making an executive decision, I decided that if a right turn could flip the body right, then a hard left would send it back to its rightful position of supine and on its back. The very next chance would be a left onto the I-70 entrance ramp. I cut it hard as I made the left turn onto the ramp. The momentum from this abrupt turn sent the cot rolling until it came to rest. I looked in the rearview mirror to see that the deceased was now lying on his stomach with a cot strapped to his back.

Next stop was the funeral home, and I was hoping and praying I didn't get pulled over for any reason. Hard to explain a corpse in back - face down on his stomach with a cot strapped to his back. I drove very carefully the rest of the way and backed into the basement garage. Mark the embalmer was already gowned and gloved up waiting for me. I yelled, "Hey, Mark! Help me get this one out!" I popped the hatch on the van, and Mark glanced in. In his best mockingly-obnoxious voice, he yelled, "AIIEEEE. A Cajun removal!!" Whatever that means. Anyway with his help, we righted the cot and the rest of the call was routine. Determined not to have any more "Cajun Removals" I went to the hardware store to get some cups to anchor the cot in so no one else would have to experience such a wild ride. Who knows what the outcome would have been had we not had the seatbelts on the cot? Seatbelts save lives. And jobs.

Death of a Dad

Systemic Mastocytosis. A rare disease claimed the life of a rare man. My daddy had been losing weight and developed a rash that wouldn't go away. The disease acted like cancer and would kill him within the year. My dad accepted his fate with bravery and humor. My mom, with the aid of my sister, was able to keep him at home until his death. The last couple of weeks were bittersweet as many of his old friends came by the house to say goodbye. Although he was in such great physical pain, he refused to accept morphine until he absolutely couldn't stand it anymore. He wanted to keep his mind clear as long as he could.

A couple of days before his death, he reluctantly agreed to fentanyl patches for the pain.The night before his death, my sister went to Dairy Queen and got him a cherry Mr. Misty. By then he was only able to have sips of water. The drugs used in his treatment had left him without an appetite. I came into the bedroom and noticed a bright red ring around his mouth from the DQ treat. I said, "Your mouth looks like a baboon's butt!" He couldn't give me his trademark knee-slapping belly laugh, but his weak grin warmed my heart just the same. I went home that night to get some sleep but came back early the next morning.

I was sitting on his bed and telling him how much I loved him and what a great father he had been. His generation wasn't much on saying "I love you," but he really didn't need to verbalize it. His actions from the time I could remember had proved his love for us daily. I was touching his face and re-telling him some of the stories he had told us kids over the years about his high jinks and the great fun he and his coworkers had enjoyed over the years. By then he was in a semi coma.

I smelled bacon frying in the kitchen, so I told him I was gonna grab some grub and return. I scarfed down the bacon and returned to the bedroom. Daddy had chosen that time to leave us. Looking back, I really think he didn't want us to have to witness his actual death. Shock, tears, and yes, relief flooded the room. We were so glad his suffering was over. My sister Nanci was dropping her kids off at school, so we waited until her return to call Dennis at the funeral home. She arrived soon and the bawling fired up again. Finally, when everyone had said their goodbyes, Dennis and I placed him tenderly on the cot and drove him to the funeral home.

Dennis did his magic, and when my mama saw him in the casket, she said his hair wasn't combed right but she liked it. For a veteran we always put a folded flag in the corner of the lid or we drape the foot panel with it. We told Dennis we preferred the flag in the lid. When I walked in for the first viewing, the flag was in the lid. It was also in the cardboard box it came in from the post office. It got the intended laugh from me, and I knew my daddy would have gotten a kick out of the gag. We then unboxed and folded the flag and placed it back in the lid.

My daddy always said that he didn't want anything fancy because the Army buddies he lost in WWII in the South Pacific didn't get any fancy caskets or expensive funerals. Well, you know how mamas are. She put him in a nice maple casket anyway. His good friend Jack preached the funeral, and he was buried in a peaceful spot in a country cemetery overlooking the Missouri River bottoms.

I can think of no higher honor than being the one to carry him out of the house and also serve as a pallbearer. My brother Dan, brother-in-law Terry and his grandsons Curtiss, Wayne, Chris and Henry all served him that day. My mama was never the same, but she did live another 25 years. She never remarried nor even dated. She said once she had the best, there was no need for the rest.

I really think that being in the funeral profession helped me cope with the terrible loss. I also feel that it made me a better funeral director because I had experienced the loss of someone dear and closer to me.

"I Think We Killed Phyllis"

We kept a dry erase board set up in the cemetery office downstairs that had the name of the deceased, visitation times, service times and burial information. If the arrangements hadn't been made yet, we would list the name only and the time of the arrangement conference. That gave anyone answering the phone the needed information at a glance for handling any inquiries. Our downstairs cemetery secretary "Phyllis" was reading the board early one morning and spied a familiar name. "Hmmmm. I went to high school with a Jack Smith. I wonder if that is him?!?" That was all it took to set the plan in motion. I dispatched "Chet" to the embalming room and set the trap for Phyllis.

"Well, Phyllis. Do you want to look at his face and see if that is your high school buddy? We can lift the sheet and show you his face and see if that is your Jack Smith." Phyllis was apprehensive, but her curiosity got the better of her. Mr. Smith had been embalmed the previous night and was lying under a sheet on a table in the prep room. We left one dim light on, and I guided Phyllis into the morgue. About the time Phyllis got to the table, Chet cried out in a spooky voice from his hiding place behind the other table, "Hi Phyllis! " as he also ruffled the bottom of the sheet covering Mr. Smith.

About the same time, I cut out the remaining light, and the morgue went pitch dark. Phyllis uttered a shriek and immediately clutched her chest and went to the floor. I quickly turned the lights back on and Chet said, "I think we killed Phyllis!" We were so afraid she had suffered a heart attack. We were very relieved when she responded as we helped her to her feet. "Was it your high school buddy?" I asked between gales of laughter. Phyllis called Chet and me some vulgar names and fled back to her post in the cemetery office. Just another morning at the funeral home. Nothing to see here, folks. Go back to your homes. The sad thing is that you can only pull a stunt like that one time on a victim. They never ever trust you around the funeral home again.

"He is Really Red!"

I don't know if it is the nature of the beast or if embalmers just needed an outlet for their pent-up stress of dealing with grieving families and being on call day in and day out, but an alarming number of them used alcohol back in the day to dull their emotions and gain temporary escape and happiness.

The embalming fluid salesmen knew that a case of beer would go far in persuading the embalmers to use their brand. One of the embalmers, Rick, was impaired the night he embalmed Mr. Jones. Like some embalmers, he was routinely DOC, or drunk on call. He was doing fine with Mr. Jones until he noticed that Mr. Jones was turning a bright shade of red. Almost neon. He immediately called the manager at home and woke him up. "He is red!" Dallas, the manager, was a bit perturbed to be woken up at 2 AM with this progress report. "Who is red?" He sleepily inquired. Rick was sobering up and said, "The body! The body is red!" Dallas said, "Finish up and we will deal with it in the morning." Rick said, "But you don't understand; he is really, really RED!!!!" Dallas calmed Rick down, and the next morning we figured out what had happened to Mr. Jones. In his impaired state, Rick had grabbed a bottle of dye instead of the Dodge Introfiant Arterial fluid.

The dye was concentrated so you were only supposed to use a capful or two to attain that rosy, lifelike appearance. Rick had used an ENTIRE bottle of the dye, and Mr. Jones was RED. OK. What to do? Well, we only had to worry about the head and the hands because after being dressed in his Sunday best, those are the only parts of the body visible to the public. One of the other embalmers, Brian, who moonlighted as an awesome body and fender man, came up with the perfect solution.

They used a can of automobile primer paint and applied it to Mr. Jones's head and hands. They then carefully applied cosmetics to make him more normal and natural.Tweak a light here and turn down a light there, and Mr. Jones made a presentable memory picture in spite of the Code Red. Here is just a bit of advice. Don't get too touchy and kissy with the corpse. You never know what the cosmetics are hiding and how many cadavers have been made up using the same brushes and double dipping into the cosmetics.

A flashback to my youthful days at Parker's. They made me go to the Merle Norman Store downtown and purchase the cosmetics. And another thing. Do you know how embarrassing it is to be sent to the Bargain Barn, a precursor of Walmart, to purchase women's hosiery and bras and panties? Yup, send the new guy.

On the other end of the alcoholic spectrum, I want to discuss the dangers of driving under the influence. David and I received a call one night to pick up a young man that had died in an unusual accident. He was so intoxicated that he thought he was on Highway 63 heading south. He actually was on Stadium Blvd which deadended at Highway 63 at that time.

He must have thought he was behind a semi tractor trailer that was moving slow. He actually was behind the trailer, but it was PARKED in the deadend and minus the tractor. There were no skid marks, and it looked like he had buried his pickup under the back axle of the trailer. I could smell the beer but couldn't for the life of me see the body anywhere. I asked the first responders where the body was. They pointed to the bed of the pickup. The force of the impact had knocked him through the back of the cab of his pickup and into the bed.

When David and I lifted him, something clanked and hit the metal bed of the pickup. David picked it up and examined it."Wow! That's the dome light from the cab. It was embedded in his head." What a waste. A 24-year-old man with his whole life ahead of him. The only blessing of that call was that he didn't actually make it to Highway 63 and kill someone else.

I quit drinking over 25 years ago and can say it was one of the best decisions of my life. One more alcohol-related story. We got a house call early one morning about 3 AM. I met "Carl" at the funeral home, and we decided to let me do the talking to the family because Carl was still slurring his words. He looked terrible. His hair was as wild as his eyes. We got to the residence, and Carl loudly ripped explosive gas as he exited the van. "Well, thanks for announcing our arrival, Carl! Remember, just keep your mouth shut and let me do the talking."

I was still kinda giggling because of the gas. You never outgrow the boyhood humor of laughing at gas. Anyway, we rolled the cot to the door with me in the lead. I introduced myself and Carl, and we entered the living room. "Mother is in the back bedroom." Carl and I made the removal without incident. As we were leaving,the family noticed Carl's disheveled appearance and glazed look in his eyes. The daughter said, "We are so very sorry to get this gentleman up at this time of night. Poor fellow - he looks so tired."

As Carl and I got back into the van, I couldn't help but chuckle. They hadn't gotten that poor gentleman up. That poor gentleman hadn't even been to bed yet. He had been drinking since he got off work. We did place the decedent in the morgue cooler so a fresher and hopefully more sober embalmer could take over.

Blood Trail

In the early days at Boone Hospital Center, you made the removals directly from the hospital bed. Dennis and I received the call one morning to pick up a lady who did not make it through her operation. We carefully wrapped her in the plastic shroud and loaded her onto the cot. We were going past the nurse's station when I noticed the first drip. A steady drip of blood was coming from the base of the cot.

We made it to the elevator and pushed the down button. The elevator must have stopped at every floor. The door would open, and Dennis and I would try to block the sight of the dripping cot from public view. By the time we reached the basement, there was a small puddle under the cot. I knew that even the most inexperienced hunter could have tracked us from the room to the van.

Not long after that debacle, Boone converted a basement room into a morgue with a refrigeration unit. The procedure then changed, and we were required to go to security and have them accompany us to the morgue and unlock it and assist if needed.

I had a favorite security officer. He obviously was uncomfortable around dead folks and would unlock the door and then head the other direction - stat.

My favorite place to remove a body from the morgue was at the hospital in Mexico, MO. Their protocol was to have the funeral home pull up at the emergency room and retrieve the key. The morgue key was attached to a foot-long stick labeled MORGUE. You would then drive to the parking garage in the basement and let yourself into the morgue to retrieve the body. The last stop was back at the ER to return the key. Reminded me of those old filling stations where you got the bathroom key from the pump jockey, and it was always attached to a wheel or cinder block so you weren't tempted to lose or steal it.

The most important part of a removal was to check the toe tag very carefully. We had a transport service that made it all the way to St. Louis with the wrong body before the mistake was discovered.

Once the body was in care of the funeral home, we used wristbands to keep track of them. Some embalmers even went so far as to use a Sharpie to label a leg. A recent law requires the use of labeling tags because of flooding that washed out some cemeteries. Nowadays the casket has an identification tube as well as ID on the body.

I assisted in the retrieval of some caskets and vaults from a cemetery in Jefferson City during the flood of 1993. Google "Harding Cemetery flood in Missouri" sometime for an extensive account of all the graves washed out there in the flood.Vernie Fountain, owner of Fountain National Academy of Embalming Skills, was instrumental in the recovery and identification of many of those bodies.

Bottom line - all bodies are labeled in some fashion these days.

Donations Are Accepted

One of the choices of disposition of human remains is donation to the anatomical board - more commonly referred to as donating one's body to science. This must be planned well in advance of the death because there is a lot of paperwork involved.

Columbia, Missouri, has a School of Medicine that accepts donations. The body is minimally embalmed and then placed in a tank to await dissection by medical students. Perhaps up to a year later, the remaining remains are cremated and returned to the family. On rare occasions, we would be called to transport a decedent to Washington University Medical Center in St. Louis to the anatomy department.

One beautiful autumn day, I was given the privilege of a road trip to St. Louis. If I played my cards right, I could kill most of the day.

I loaded up the body and made it to St. Louis right around lunch time. I had never made a trip to Wash U but found it easily and even figured out which loading dock to park at. I unloaded the client and proceeded up the ramp into the bowels of the sprawling medical complex.

No signs directed me to the anatomy department, so I started asking employees. I was ignored twice, and a third person didn't know where it was and didn't offer to find me someone who did. Did I mention it was lunch time?

I happened to see a sign with directions to the cafeteria. I started to wheel my gurney in that direction. It was amazing how helpful they became. Didn't take long for an employee to say, "Hey! What are you doing? " I immediately found a good samaritan who would rather see the body reach the anatomy department than the cafeteria.

After gaining entrance to the anatomy department, I was in for a sight that shocked even a jaded undertaker. A device was placed around the decedent's head, and she was wrapped in a clear shroud and hung on a conveyor-like device that resembled the contraption you see at a dry cleaners when they are retrieving your clothing. She was assigned a number and then whisked away into the room-sized, walk-in cooler and hung there to await her turn with the medical students. If you ever saw the movie *Coma,* you can visualize the scene. My one word description of what I witnessed that day? HIDEOUS. I certainly wouldn't want someone I loved disposed of like that. To each his own, but I think if folks knew exactly what donation entails, they might opt for cremation. Now bear in mind, that happened over 20 years ago, and their procedures might have changed. Or not.

Cushy Job = Easy Money

"Hey, Easy Money!" "Man I wish I had your job!" "Must be rough!" At least one visitation a week I would have remarks like that hurled in my general direction. Back in the eighties at Memorial, my hours were 8 to 5 and on call every other night and every other weekend. If a visitation was scheduled, we were to leave at 3 pm but be back at 5 to cover visitation. So basically you would work a 12-hour day. Doesn't sound so bad, does it? Stand around in a suit and act like you are genuinely glad to see everyone that comes through the front door.

Well, in those days, smoking was allowed everywhere at any time. There were nights when I would open the door to admit a guest and see clouds of smoke hurling out the door. The ashtrays would have to be emptied at least once and maybe twice during a visitation. Death makes folks edgy and nervous, and nicotine was the preferred antidote. It got so bad that Mike and I would keep a cigar handy to puff in self defense. Folks who had normal jobs would see us "standing around" in a suit and think we were being paid "the big bucks" basically for looking pretty. We would watch the clock anxiously waiting for 9 pm. The end of visitation. But wait. What's this? A car pulls up at 8:50 pm, and three people get out. They wander back to the family and talk another 30 minutes. Ok. 9:30 pm. Not too bad, but since the funeral is set for 10 am the next morning, we need to "move over" before we can leave. By move over, I mean relocate the casket along with 30 potted plants and cut floral arrangements, complete with flower racks, into the chapel from the visitation room. Then run the vacuum sweeper and clean the restrooms, including dumping the trash and scrubbing the toilets. Then, maybe then, you can leave. By then it's about 10:30 pm, and you head home.

First thing you do is lose the suit. You stink of second-hand smoke and decide to shower before bed. You need to unwind, so you catch the last of the Late Show. You are finally relaxed enough to crawl into bed. Your head hits the pillow, and you are just about out when BRRRIIINNGG the phone brings you back to the reality that you are on call and about ready to extend that 12-hour day. A couple or three hours later, you finally make it back home and decide to forget the unwind part and go straight to bed. If all goes well, you might catch 4 hours of sleep before getting back to the funeral home to make sure the cars look presentable for the morning funeral. It wasn't rocket science, but the work could be both mentally and physically tiring.

Every interview for a funeral home position includes a question about your ability and fitness to be able to lift a set amount of weight. My stock answer to this question is, "Hey! I lift 300 pounds every time I get up from a chair!" I am ashamed to say that once in awhile I would use the "faux rise" whenever someone was leaving a visitation. This patented move was performed by grabbing the arms of the chair and doing a half-hearted attempt at getting up- but not quite achieving lift off. The thought behind this move was that the person was already on their way out and maybe they thought I got up to greet them.

I googled "funeral director salary" one time. They must have surveyed union directors in New York City. Even with 4O years' experience, the pay was at least 10-15 thousand less than the "average" quote given. No.We don't do it for the lavish lifestyle it affords. Funeral service is a calling. Rant over. More jocularity coming.

Funeral Arrangements

Arrangement conferences were a minefield where you had to walk the fine line between friend, biographer, grief counselor and salesman. I was ok with the first 3 roles but would starve to death if I depended on a sales career. You take a person on the worst day of their life and try to help them make sense of something that makes no sense.

I always preferred a one-on-one arrangement. Because I was more of a friend than a predator, the family didn't need a protector from the greedy undertaker. With one on one, I could quickly establish a rapport and really listen while the person vented, or provide answers to their questions. The most difficult arrangements were when a person would bring in their friends and extended family. A simple question, such as when and where did you get married, could turn into a 15-minute discussion that slowed down the process and just added more painful time to their visit.

I would get the statistical information for the death certificate and then some added biographical background for the obituary. I would show them the caskets and explain all the prices and then step out to process the obituary and allow them some time to discuss what they could afford and how they would pay for it.

Before word processors and computers, a single mistake on an obit would lead to either retyping the entire thing or much white-out. Some families would concentrate on a misplaced semicolon or a missing comma while others would just flat out forget to mention a surviving brother or sister.

We always tried to collect at least half of the total before the funeral because we knew that once that body was in the ground, the funeral bill would become much less of a priority.

Back when I started, there was basically one musical option for the service. We would hire an organist to play a prelude 10 minutes before the funeral, let the family pick out a couple or 3 songs and then a postlude. You were guaranteed to hear *Amazing Grace, Old Rugged Cross* or *In the Garden*. Later came the cassette tapes which were difficult to cue to the correct song and then the wonderful addition of CD's.

These days, the sky is the limit. If it is on YouTube, the assembled crowd can watch the video of the song and sing along if they wish. Technology these days allows the funeral to be webcast anywhere in the world so relatives in other countries can virtually attend the funeral.

Funerals are casual affairs these days, and anyone with the guts or nerve can get up and "preach" a funeral.

I have learned to vet the musical choices because of some unfortunate incidents where a "live" version of a song was played which included the foul language of the performer.

Funerals have come a long way in 40 years from simple religion-based goodbyes to multimedia celebrations of life. More and more people are choosing to leave the body itself out of the mix and have a memorial service at a later date that will accommodate more people and fit into their busy schedules. Well, funerals are for the living after all.

Two Guys and A Hearse

Dennis and I shared the same weekends on at Memorial and would always dream about what it would be like to work for ourselves. By 1997, around the time a conglomerate corporate funeral chain purchased Memorial, Dennis began to seriously make plans to open his own funeral home. I was allowed to join him in his venture. He provided all the capital and assumed all the risk. There was only room for 2 in his lifeboat. We determined that we could provide a more personal service at a much more reasonable price. He bought an embalming service on the edge of town and converted it into a funeral home with a large chapel.

One of the names we came up with for the new funeral home was "2 Guys and a Hearse"; while catchy, we opted for Nilson Funeral Home.Things were rough at the start, but when the other funeral homes saw that we were going to succeed and not actually hurt them, we reached a cease fire and peacefully coexisted with them.

He opened a trade embalming service to pay the bills until the funerals started rolling in. Dennis and I were basically on call 24/7 but were small enough we could put a sticky note on the door if we wanted to go out for a "business" breakfast or lunch. The homey atmosphere also lent itself to regular visits from old friends in the business and embalming supply salesmen.

One such regular was Tim, a gentleman who had owned the funeral home in a nearby town. He would regularly regale us with tales from his numerous decades in the business. Our chapel was large, but the small arrangement room, which doubled as our lunchroom, was located across from the restrooms.

I was making arrangements one morning when I saw Tim pull up. I heard him enter the building, and then I heard the men's room door open and shut. He didn't realize I was arranging a funeral when he kicked the bathroom door open and came running around the corner. "Hey, Pal. Where's the plunger?" He bellowed before he saw the family I was meeting with. Before I could tell him, he backed out quietly and I heard the front door softly close. Nothing to see here, folks. Just another typical morning at Nilson Funeral Home.

Tim was also known for waiting for the American Legion rifle team to shoot their 3 volleys and then announcing, "They missed me." I looked forward to his visits as he was a wealth of funeral knowledge and stories.

Another legendary story involved his brother driving a hearse during a funeral procession. He was multitasking and watching the Chiefs game on his portable TV when he hit a dog that had wandered into the road. The show must go on. They made it to the cemetery and conducted the graveside service.

Another favorite story told by Tim was how his brother who also worked at the family funeral home was closing a casket. Some families prefer the casket to be closed before the funeral service. Tim's brother had closed the lid and was cranking it down to seal it. When he straightened up, he realized he had sealed the lid shut on his tie. He was immobilized until he could uncrank the casket. Tim is gone now, but his stories will live on.

Back in Bed, Boys

Dennis and I were sitting in the lounge one afternoon and got a call for a service that I had never even thought of. A poor lady in her 70's had a son who was in his mid 40's and dying of cancer. She calmly explained that her son had fallen out of bed and that she couldn't afford the cost of an ambulance to come out and put her son back in bed. Of course, we were glad to help her. We drove to the house and lifted the poor gentleman off the floor and gently placed him back in bed. I sincerely hope that he was out of it enough not to realize that a couple of undertakers were putting him back in bed. We did this at no cost to her. He lived another week or two, and the next time we came to his house, we brought him back with us.

I Know You!

Dennis and I worked all the visitations and funerals at Nilson Funeral Home. Folks would start dropping by at 5 pm after they got off work and trickle in until 9 pm. We would always play some background music to set the mood for the first viewing. More often than not, we would play the soundtrack to the movie *Titanic*. Its melancholy instrumentals would set the tone and if they weren't crying by the time Celine Dion cut loose with "My Heart Will Go On," then we would fire up the classical stuff with Pachelbel Canon in D to help them release their emotions.

It had been a long day and was getting longer because some parents had turned their 6-year-old child loose while they entered the chapel to view the body and visit the family. I could hear that kid running around in the lounge and just acting like kids will do when they are out of sight of their parents. The little heathen was stomping on the floors, fanning the bathroom doors, and raiding the candy bowl. He was yanking cushions off the sofa and throwing them all over the floor. In my mind I was thinking about throwing him into the prep room for a minute or two and see if that would calm him. Not wishing for a police visit or a lawsuit, I decided to just wait him out. Surely a parent would emerge soon and put an end to his mischief.

I had just admitted an elderly couple into the chapel when here came that kid running around the corner looking for more things to tear up. He stopped when he saw me giving him the stink eye. Before I could say a word, he looked me directly in the eye and loudly announced: "I know you! You're a horse's (behind)! " I was shocked into silence. I had two thoughts. First of all, how did he know I am a horse's (behind) and second, who taught him that vulgar phrase to begin with?

After he made his somewhat accurate pronouncement, he gleefully took off into the chapel and into the custody of his parents.

Raising a sassy 7 year old of my own, I have a whole new appreciation for what parents go through when they take their progeny into public places.

Surrounded By Love

Dennis and I received a residence call one beautiful fall afternoon. I guess you would call it an Indian summer day because although it was late October, the temperature was in the low 80's. We were told by the caller that we could take our time responding because more of the family was still gathering at the house to say goodbye. Dennis and I did take our time and just enjoyed the nice 45 minute drive out into the countryside.

The house sat off the road quite a ways and had a nice wraparound porch in front. Cars were parked on both sides of the road and all over the yard. That had always been a pet peeve of mine. You need to either leave room or make room for the undertaker's rig. It is sometimes difficult to negotiate a cot across a debris-strewn lawn or navigate a loaded cot between parked cars. Just remember to allow the undertaker a handicapped parking space. Please and thank you.

We backed up as close as we could to the porch, and I started mentally counting all the folks there. I gave up at 27. Brothers. Sisters. Sons. Daughters. Grandkids. Nieces. Nephews. All were gathered on that porch. I had never seen so much love in one small place before. I was thinking that if there were that many people outside the house, how many were gathered inside around the deceased?

We left the cot in the van until we determined where the decedent was and to map out our way through the crowd and onto the porch. We made our introductions and then asked exactly where Mr. Smith was currently located. The daughter looked incredulously at me and said, "Right there!" as she pointed at a man in overalls sitting comfortably in a wooden Adirondack chair on the front porch. I asked again where I could locate the dead man.

"Right there!" She pointed again and said louder. I looked a little closer. The dead man was sitting in the chair, eyes wide open staring vacantly.

He had a couple of grandbabies crawling around in his lap and assorted other kinfolk hugging and petting him. Instead of revulsion at this sight, I knew I was seeing primal love and grief all mixed together in a beautiful picture that I can still see in my mind these 20 years later. If a person could have their choices of ways to die, I would pick this one. He had obviously suffered from a terminal illness, but during his last hours on earth he was literally surrounded by love and all the fruits of his labor.

I hated to interrupt this intimate and wonderful moment. Dennis and I gently loaded him into our van and took him into our care. I felt privileged that the family had trusted us to help them with this ancient and sacred ritual.

Breaking the Color Barrier

The funeral business was probably one of the very last professions to become integrated. The 1964 Civil Rights Act, while sweeping as it was, could not force black folks to use a white funeral home and vice versa. In Columbia, you had the Memorial Funeral Home and Parker Funeral Service catering to white clientele, while Stuart P. Parker Funeral Home, later bought by Harold Warren and named Warren Funeral Chapel, handled all the black funerals.

Stuart P. Parker Funeral Home operated out of the historic former home of Boone County, Missouri's world famous musician Blind Boone. Boone was a blind and black gentleman that could make a piano sound like a tornado storming through the building. I was amazed throughout my career in the 70's and 80's and even until the mid 90's that blacks exclusively used the black-owned parlor, and whites exclusively used the white-owned parlors.

To Dennis's credit and also to the chagrin of the black funeral home owner, Dennis hired Roland, a husky and loveable, black gentleman to assist with funerals and sell funeral plans for Nilson. This got us a foot in the door and allowed us to serve a few members of the black community as well. Roland was nothing if not loyal and punctual, showing up at 8 AM every morning in a full suit and carrying his trademark briefcase. Roland was so laid back that you could be carrying on a conversation that would turn one sided because he could fall asleep mid sentence.

Physically, he resembled Cedric the Entertainer. I'm not sure if Roland had some undiagnosed heart affliction, but he died suddenly and way too young. I will always remember him fondly not just for his personality but for his helping Nilson Funeral Home to break the color barrier in Columbia.

Nowadays, Millard Funeral Home has purchased the black funeral home and a couple of the white ones, and finally the funeral business in Columbia is integrated.

Catholic Funerals

Catholic funerals can be confusing to Protestant funeral directors. Especially if the directors are distracted or napping or bored. Dennis had hired a former sales counselor from Memorial named John. John was a tall, skinny, good-humored fellow who had two traits that served him well in the profession. He was perpetually nervous and worried. We used John once in awhile as a third hand on funeral services when we needed someone to drive family or pallbearers.

Most all Catholic services are held at the church usually at 10 AM. They are automatic affairs that require little of the funeral director except at the very beginning and the end. We would bring the casket into the foyer where it was blessed by the priest and then covered with a pall, or large cloth the size of a tablecloth. The priest leads it with pallbearers alongside and family following into the sanctuary. Once started, the service is on autopilot until the end when the directors come up to the front. The priest then leads the casket, pallbearers and family back out to the foyer where the pall is removed. The casket is then rolled out of the church to the waiting hearse. Pretty basic stuff. Until it isn't.

After getting the service started, the funeral directors exile themselves to the "cry room." This is a soundproof room at the back of the sanctuary with blinds and glass where the services can be seen and heard but not disturbed by obnoxious children or crying babies.The audio of the service is fed into the room. It is a perfect place for the undertakers to hide out and relax or nap until the long service is over.

On this particular day, Dennis, John and I were stationed in the cry room and doing an excellent job of not paying attention. We missed our cues and had no idea where in the service the priest was. I tried to be helpful and mentioned I thought I had heard a couple of songs and a prayer or two. Dennis agreed. Suddenly, we saw the priest come down to the head of the casket with a couple of his robed helpers. Knowing there was a good chance it was over, we sent John up to the front as a sort of weather balloon to test the waters. We were not going to get burned this time like we did that one time when Chet had distracted us in the cry room, and the priest had to send a pallbearer back there to flush us out.

I can't remember exactly what Chet was doing, but it had our full attention when we heard someone knocking on the cry room door. AWKWARD! John was already halfway up to the front when Dennis and I realized that it was the break for communion and not the end of the service. It was too late to stop John, so we let the scene play out to its improvisational conclusion.

John reached the front of the chapel. The priest eyed John and gave a slight shake of his head. Translation: "No! What are you doing up here?!?" Yes. I read all that with his "no no nod."

Thankfully, Dennis and I had stayed back in the cry room so we only had one dog in that fight. John stood next to the priest and clasped his hands in his best imitation of an undertaker.The priest then ignored John who stood stoically up there until communion was over. He then slowly walked to a side aisle and returned to us in the cry room. The cry room was muffling the laughter of Dennis and me. John was not a happy camper and felt we had betrayed him.

He got over it, and 15 minutes later when the service was actually over, we all went to our battle stations and the service ended without further incident. The priest never mentioned our faux paus and neither did the family. They probably chalked it up to those crazy Protestants not understanding their rituals.

Dennis and I learned a valuable lesson that day and vowed to pay better attention to a service in progress. John got over the shame and trauma and lived to work another Catholic service.

Death of a Wife

We knew a couple of weeks after we got married, that this day would come eventually. At age 24, I married a 19 year old. She had been diagnosed with juvenile diabetes at age 9 and was on 2 insulin shots a day. The blood test for our marriage revealed a false positive for an STD. That was the good news.

The bad news is that it revealed she had systemic lupus, an autoimmune disease that attacks the vital organs. She was given an estimated life expectancy of 15 more years which seemed like a lifetime to a young couple.

Over the years, Mary would be hospitalized for various complications of both of her diseases. The relentless attack of the lupus on her lungs and kidneys and the severe diabetes eventually took their toll.

Mary faced her debilitating illnesses with good humor, bravery and a deep faith in God. She suffered a sharp decline right after Thanksgiving in 2004. We placed her on home Hospice on Christmas Eve that year. The beautiful part of such a lingering death is that you are able to tell your partner exactly how much you love them and discuss the deep meaningful things that sometimes get lost in the mediocrity of day-to-day living.

Mary not only lined out her funeral wishes, she told me in no uncertain terms to remarry a Christian because she knew it was not in my DNA to survive such a loss on my own. About a week before her death, I let Dennis know that I needed to stay home with her until it was over. Eventually, hospice gave us morphine to make her comfortable. The night before her death, she fell out of the bed about 10:30 PM.

I lifted her back into bed and her last words to me were, "I think I fell." She then lapsed into a peaceful coma. I called my preacher and his wife, and they came and sat with me. Around 3 AM she took her last breath. She died about 4 months shy of our 25th anniversary. I called Dennis, and he came right over. We gently placed her onto the cot, and I drove her to the funeral home. I knew Dennis would be in shortly to work his magic. I went back home and that was the hardest part of the entire ordeal. Going back into the house knowing that she ain't there and is never gonna be there again. It hits you between the eyes like a brick.

After church that morning, I went home and just laid down on the couch and cried. I highly recommend that to anyone who experiences the death of someone close. You don't need an audience. You just need to haul off and get some good old-fashioned grieving done. Alone. With a good cry. I think I cried myself to sleep that night.

I had already pre-arranged everything; in fact, Mary had written down her wishes as well. I did need to make a trip to the florist. I was determined to spend the Social Security death benefits on flowers. Yes, Social Security will pay a surviving spouse $255. That might pay some of the
sales tax on funeral merchandise. And yes, friends, caskets, vaults and tangible goods are all taxed.

I went to see Bob, the manager at the local grocery department's flower shop. We knew each other pretty well. I said, "Hey Bob. I need to get my wife some flowers!" He said, "Sure, Don. What are you thinking? A spring basket? A vase of roses? What's the occasion?"

I looked Bob in the eye and said, "What do you have in funeral sprays?" Bob said, "Huh?" I matter of factly uttered, "My wife just died." Ouch. Bob knew me well enough to enjoy my morbid sense of humor, but this one caught him off guard.

Dennis did a wonderful job, and Mary looked years younger and healthier. The funeral went well.
I was able to close the casket, and I drove the hearse to the cemetery. I also helped carry her to the grave. Instead of letting her casket spray rot on the grave, I let every woman and girl there grab a rose or two. Long story short, Mary had told her wishes to my preacher's wife. She knew a good Christian girl in Arkansas named Robbie that met Mary's high standards for me. Happy ending for me is that I had 25 wonderful years with Mary, and I have been blessed with Robbie for over 14 years now. God is good. Hang onto Him, and He will get you through all of the trials of life and death.

Flashback

Flashback. I had gotten my BA in political science with no job in sight. I tried a semester of Journalism School and finally decided in December of 1977 to just get on with life and get a job. Any job.

My Aunt Betty worked at the Cancer Hospital, and I soon found out it's not what you know but who you know. I was hired on as a CNA with on-the-job training. The hours were less than desirable - 11 PM to 7:30 AM. As a CNA, I was given the jobs that no one else would do. I remember once being given the task of taking a man's temperature. At 3 AM in a semi darkened room, I realized due to his esophageal cancer, the temp had to be taken rectally. I made one attempt.

As I withdrew the thermometer, I realized I hadn't used a rectal one. I made an executive decision and decided I was not going to put him or me through that again. His chart would read, "Temp. 98.6." Yes, folks. You get what you pay for. That was the caliber of the help. What did you expect for $2.88 an hour?

Another time I was to give an amputee his bath. He had no arms nor legs, so I lifted him into a chair that was supposed to crank down into the bathtub. I must have bumped the quick release because the seat sank quickly into the water, and he tumbled into the tub. He was helplessly bobbing around in the water. I apologized all over the place as I lifted him out of the water. He looked at me fearfully and said, "That's all right, partner. Just dry me off and get me in some clean clothes. I won't tell anyone."

I guess what happens in the bathing room at the State Cancer Hospital stays in the bathing room at the State Cancer Hospital.

The hardest part of the shift was just before dawn. I could barely stay awake. Another task I was given was to shave a man that was obviously in a lot of pain and on his way out. I asked the nurse why "we" were shaving this unfortunate soul, and the answer she gave me still haunts me. "So he will look good for the undertaker."

After about 3 months in the medical field, I was invited by a lawn care customer to work at his funeral home. I figured at least at the funeral home I couldn't harm the patients.

I Kilt Him With a Pair of Scissors

"I kilt him with a pair of scissors cause they took away my guns." Bet you don't hear that very often during a normal conversation at work. Let me go back about an hour before this statement. Jimmy and I had caught the residential call to pick up a gentleman from up in an extremely rural and remote area of Ozark County, Missouri. We were given some general directions and headed north out of Arkansas into the beautiful Ozarks of southern Missouri. Jimmy and I enjoyed a leisure conversation until we had to pinpoint the location of the death which wound up being at the end of a pig trail off of a rural highway.

As we crept up the crude trail, we passed a couple of abandoned cars and finally arrived at a shack sitting in the middle of the weed-infested yard. The widow sat in a lawn chair and greeted us cheerfully. "You fellers from the funeral home?" We affirmed that we weren't Mormon missionaries or salesmen and introduced ourselves. I noticed Jimmy shake her hand and then quickly wipe it on a tree. Apparently, the old gal, who put me in the mind of Granny on the *Beverly Hillbillies*, had gotten some poop on her hands either from taking care of the Mister or from her own bad hygiene.

I declined the handshake, and we followed her into the "house." The living room looked like it was just on the verge of "hoard." She told us to watch out for copperheads because she had "kilt" one very recently. Apparently, some hunters had trespassed on her land, and she had brandished her pistol and threatened them. They called the "laws" on her; the "laws" took her gun. "I kilt him with a pair of scissors. The laws took my gun." I made a mental note right then and there not to mess with anyone who kills venomous snakes with scissors.

She pointed to the other room and said, "He's in there." The bedroom was just about large enough for the "bed," a stained mattress on the floor. The single light socket hanging over the "bed" was missing a bulb, but Jimmy was able to warn me not to step on the rather large lizard that scampered away as I went to help roll the Mister into a sheet so we could carry him into the living room. I got distracted reading the newspaper that served as wallpaper in the room.

"You fellers want a drink?" Jimmy and I spoke as one, "No, thanks!" As we wheeled the gentleman into the yard, the widow's preacher showed up. He had one of those burr haircuts, and she grabbed him in a fierce hug and rubbed her hands through his hair. Jimmy and I had to bite our lips to keep from laughing at the thought of that preacher with his poop-smeared hair. We excused ourselves and loaded the dead man into the van.

We slowly drove back out of the pig trail and noticed the "laws" parked at the end of the trail. They said, "How was she?" We then realized why there was no coroner or law enforcement at the scene of the home death. I honestly think they were trying to avoid any further confrontation with this loose cannon. We assured them that everything was fine and the deceased was in our care. We couldn't wait to get to a gas station to wash our hands and get something to drink. I don't think I have ever laughed that hard that long before or since.

That old gal endeared herself to me. She had me at "I kilt him with a pair of scissors." You simply cannot make this stuff up!

Miss a Turn

You get to know preachers pretty well when cooped up in the front end of a hearse on the way to a burial. After the service in the chapel, the preacher is given the option of driving his own car or riding with the undertaker to the cemetery where the brief committal service will take place. This time the burial was going to be about a half hour drive north of Mountain Home.

"James," while not a preacher per se, conducts a lot of funerals for church members. He does a fine job as evidenced by the number of folks who request him. On this day I was driving the hearse, and James was riding shotgun. We were catching up with each other, and then he started to reminisce about the time he took a hot air balloon ride. I was laughing at the humorous story when I glanced in the rearview mirror and noticed to my shock and awe that the 15 cars in the procession were nowhere in sight. They had correctly turned off Highway 5 onto the road that would take us to the cemetery.

I said, "Uh oh, James. I think we lost them." I knew we must turn around, so I pulled into the Volunteer Fire Department parking lot and headed back south. I made the correct turn, and thankfully all fifteen cars had pulled over and were patiently waiting for the hearse to retake the lead.

I pulled back in front of them and led the way on to the cemetery. When we stopped at the grave, James and I got out of the hearse and approached the family. Expecting the worst, I cowardly threw James under the bus. I told the daughter, "I am so sorry, but James and I were talking and just missed the turn off." Bless that daughter's heart! She said, "That's OK, Don. Mama likes to ride, and I am sure she enjoyed that little detour." Wow! Another family from a more northern clime might have threatened to sue the funeral home for emotional distress. Cooler heads prevailed, and I am sure Mama's last ride will make it into her family's fond memory banks. It certainly did mine. You can't control death, but you can certainly control how you react to it.

Chow Time

Most of the time when a family opts for cremation, they will wait for a convenient time for family members to gather for the memorial service. Then they will either take the cremated remains home with them to put in a place of honor or divide them up among family members. Another popular option is scattering them. Maybe the decedent had a favorite hunting place or fishing hole. Perhaps there were favorite memories of the ocean.

Most cemeteries offer either niches in a columbarium or in ground burial if the goal is a marked spot for families to visit from time to time. One popular option is a scattering garden where the cremated remains are placed and commingled with other cremains and their name placed on a common plaque.

Our story today involves a scattering garden in a rural cemetery. The gentleman had just received a nice service at the church, and we then proceeded on to the cemetery and to their scattering garden. The bucolic setting included a restful, grassy area bordered on one side by a cow pasture. The cows were doing what cows do and seemed marginally interested in what we were up to.

The preacher and I walked to the garden followed by the family and friends. I held the guest of honor in the black utility urn that is used for scattering. No need for an expensive urn with this disposition. The deceased gentleman was a veteran, and we had military honors complete with the folding of the flag, the military chaplain and the gun salute.

Following the gun salute, I opened the urn and removed the plastic bag containing the cremated remains. As I emptied the bag into the garden, the wind shifted and blew a slight cloud of dust toward the gathered bovines. They started sniffing the air and started heading towards the fence. It suddenly hit me what had gotten them so interested in our funeral. Cremated remains are nothing but pulverized bones. Bone meal, if you will. They thought it was chow time.

Very few, if any, of the spectators realized why the cows were gathered and paying such attention. Snorting a little stray calcium never hurt anyone.

This reminds me of the time I had processed some cremains on a Sunday morning before church. After cremation, all that is left is the fragile bone structure. This is raked into a pan and then checked by magnet for any metal that would damage the processor. The bones are then pulverized and placed into the urn. I was running late, as usual, and slipped into the pew next to my wife Robbie. She immediately noticed a "crumb" on my tie and whispered, "Hmm. Had a Hardee's biscuit, did we?" as she picked the "crumb" off.

Before it left my tie, I noticed that the "crumb" was a pulverized chunk of bone. Now before you get all freaked out about germs etc., remember that this crumb had been subjected to 1600 degrees for 2 hours.

Pulling cremated remains in the summer was a hot, sweaty and dirty job. We had one embalmer who would retreat to the walk-in morgue cooler after a cremation processing and hang out in there until he cooled off. My first cremation at this particular funeral home was going well. I had pressed all the buttons at the right time. I stepped out of the cremation building and gazed at the stack. If there were visible emissions such as smoke coming out, we had to tweak the knobs and buttons until the air mixture was right. This time there was no black smoke rolling out, so I went back to close the door to the building. It was safe to leave it for the duration. Just as I entered the building, I heard a loud explosion that sounded like a pacemaker blowing up. Leaving a pacemaker in was a big no no. The battery could blow up and damage the retort. I was spinning and sweating and in a panic when the cemetery grounds supervisor came around the corner laughing at my expense.   Apparently, he had thrown a handful of gravel on the metal roof of the building. Makes a terrible racket. Made his day. You just can't trust anybody.

Snakehead Showdown

I hold a healthy fear of snakes. I don't go out of my way to look for one, and if I see one in person, I will head in the opposite direction. Todd, the manager of the Arkansas funeral home, is deathly afraid of snakes. I think he was bitten by one in his youth and still carries the trauma of that incident.

Todd let everyone at the funeral home know of his phobia. Of course, we were understanding. We understood how to get some cheap entertainment at his expense. The cemetery grounds men would kill the odd snake and leave it on the parking lot right under Todd's driver side door. We would find realistic rubber snakes to hide in places that he was sure to tread. You know. Harmless fun. Well, an older gentleman named Pete worked part time for the funeral home. He had even gotten his embalmer's license in his 60's.

Pete had a wonderful and dry sense of humor. One day he showed me an actual copperhead snake head that had been preserved. That thing was vicious looking. Eyes open, jaws agape with fangs bared ready to strike. Hmmm. How could we use this artifact to full advantage?

The perfect opportunity fell right into my hands. I asked Todd if he would help me dress a lady. In the sack of clothing, I placed the copperhead head on top. We headed toward the prep room, and I could barely contain my glee. I had wished I could video this but didn't want to tip him off. We got to the prep room, and I handed the sack to Todd and stood back to watch the fun. He reached into the sack and the first thing he grabbed was the copperhead head.

To my amazement and chagrin, he simply one handed it and held it about 6 inches from his face. It wasn't until he realized that what he was staring at was staring back at him that the fun began. He thought it was jewelry or a brooch to pin on the dress. When his eyes met the snake eyes and fangs, I saw a performance that held me mesmerized as well. Todd turned pale and clammy. He went through all 5 stages of grief in about 30 seconds. First, there was denial. Then anger. The bargaining came next. With much cursing I might add...There were a couple of seconds of depression and then came acceptance.

This all was accomplished with much heart clutching, hyperventilating,visceral, primal, terror-driven fear.

I think honestly if I hadn't been cowering in the corner and laughing so hard, he might have jumped into my arms.Todd jumped up and down and shrieked like a little girl. He then threw the snake head at me. Once he recovered his composure, his immediate reaction was revenge. He speed dialed the cemetery grounds supervisor. "Hey you (expletive deleted) sick (expletive deleted), where the (expletive deleted) did you get this (expletive deleted) snake head?"

I couldn't let Ronnie take the heat for this one. So I did the only right thing to do. I threw Pete under the bus. "Hey, Todd. It was Pete that gave me that snake head. I am sooo sorry. I didn't realize you are THAT afraid of snakes." Todd's blood pressure slowly returned to normal and his curses slowed down. At one point I honestly thought he was going to need treatment. Sort of an anti-dead snake head venom shot or something.

Looking back, it was a pretty ornery thing to do, but you have to get your kicks where you can. Funeral homes don't have to be somber and dull. Throw a snake head into the mix once in awhile.

Military Honors

Military honors are an important and, in fact, vital part of a veteran's funeral. We usually try to contact the branch of service, be it Army, Navy, Air Force or Marines, to arrange the honors team to perform the service. The honors consist of folding and presenting the flag, a rifle salute and taps. Those young men and women are top notch and do an excellent job.

Sometimes we also use the local American Legion and VFW guys. These gentlemen are old and getting older. The gun salute where 7 men fire a volley of three is supposed to sound like 3 single shots but more often than not sounds like a quail hunt. Ba Ba Boom. I don't know if it is because some of them start drinking an hour or two before the service or if it is just their age. The military does its part after the preacher is through.

On one particular occasion, the Legion guys were waiting for their part, and the preacher was about halfway through his committal service when the commander's cell phone went off. Most folks immediately try to silence this intrusion. This day the commander had his phone velcroed onto his wrist. He placed his wrist up to his mouth and loudly announced, "Hello?!? Yes. Uh huh. Well, yes. Hey! I am at a (Lord's name in vain) funeral! Yeah. Funeral. I'm gonna have to call you back." At least the preacher tried to talk over him during this profane conversation.

Back in the day, "Taps" was played by a live bugler. In the late eighties, they transitioned to a CD recording of Taps. They now have a sound chip in a fake bugle so the faux bugler can render Taps. On this particular day the "bugler" hit the button on his bugle and Taps started. The trouble was that the bugle was still at waist level. After the first "Ta Ta Ta," he put the bugle to his lips. Reminded me of the old ventriloquist who could drink a glass of water while singing the Star Spangled Banner. Bless their hearts. Those guys and gals try and give it their best. In fact, they did give their best back when it counted. I thank them all for their service to our country in times of war and peace. God bless our veterans and active service members everywhere.

Locked Out

The funeral service was set for 10 AM at a rural church about an hour's drive from the funeral home. Beautiful spring day, only a couple of racks of flowers, and Dick as my helper. Life was going good that day. If a funeral could be routine, this was gonna be it. My buddy Dick and I loaded up the casket in the hearse and placed the flowers and racks in the flower van and headed out about 7:30 AM. We pulled into the church parking lot about 8:30, and I was relieved to see that the grave had been dug and the vault company was there setting up the tent, chairs and lowering device.

Visions of the potluck dinner after the service were dancing in my head as I sailed out of the hearse. Dick already had gotten out of the van and was unloading flower racks. We headed for the church building and...pulled on a locked door. No problem. Someone would be by soon to unlock the church. I sauntered back to the hearse and pulled on the back door. Hmmm. Locked. Oh well. I'll just open the driver side door and unlock it. Locked. Locked ?? Locked!!

The hearse was locked up tighter than a 24-hour gas station kiosk in East St. Louis, with the key still in the ignition. I must have bumped the lock button when I jumped out.

I asked Dick if we kept a spare key under the fender well. Negative. Well, it's an hour back to the funeral home. The key was a 2-hour round trip away, and it was then 8:30. Thank God for cell phones. I called the funeral home, and they dispatched Phil, an older but Chicago-bred, fast-driving funeral director, to head my way with a key. I sent Dick in the flower van to try to meet him halfway.

That left me. And Mrs. Smith. Locked in the hearse. The good news is someone showed up with a key to the church about 9. I hauled the flower racks and flowers into the church and got them set up. That left me 40 minutes till show time. My buddy Dick was on the key run, so I was left to face the music. I did some heavy praying.

The family showed up about 9:30 and I had to tell them the sorry news that Mom was locked in the hearse. They took this news graciously, and I stationed myself at the church door handing out programs and pointing out the guestbook. Dick came flying low into the parking lot about 9:56. We grabbed the pallbearers and released Mama from the hearse. She arrived on time and was wheeled in

place in front of the assembled guests. Sometimes things work out well in spite of the clumsy actions of very human directors. The family was

pleased and even alluded to the fact that Mom was a practical joker and probably had something to do with the locked hearse. As an added bonus, Dick and I were invited to the potluck. Thank God for cell phones and good non-litigious, genuine Arkansas natives who keep calm and look for the good in a bad situation.

Are You Ready for Some Football?

It was October of 1993, and the Kansas City Chiefs were still contenders under the guidance of aging quarterback Joe Montana. We hadn't been that excited about the Chiefs in a long time, and this was before they would choke in the playoffs as usual. Dennis and I got the residential call during the end of halftime and got to the home right about the time the 3rd quarter was ending. We knocked on the door and received no answer. Then tried the doorbell and the elderly gentleman answered.

The Chiefs game was blasting from the TV in the living room, and Montana had just thrown one of his trademark "look downfield this way and throw downfield that way" passes that connected with Marcus Allen. All living eyes in the room were on that game. I laid my bulky early 90's model cell phone down, and Dennis and I proceeded to the bedroom to take Mrs. Jones into our care. Mr. Jones stayed in the living room with the game while we tucked Mrs. Jones onto the cot.

We got permission for embalming and set up an appointment for the following day to make the final arrangements. As we slowly and gently exited the house, Montana made another exciting completion. We hustled to the van to try to catch the final moments of the fourth quarter on the radio. I had made it back onto the highway when I told Dennis we had to go back. "Why?" I had to admit that I had been distracted by the game and left my cell phone at the home of the deceased.

We pulled back into his driveway and I rang the bell again. "Decide to watch the rest of the game? "Mr. Jones smiled and asked me. I had to admit to him that I had left my cell phone on his end table. Again, neither of our eyes left that game as I retrieved my phone. When you finally have a winning team with legendary players, it is hard to concentrate on work. Mr. Jones was a fan. He understood...

I'm Not Done Yet

Funerals are kind of like weddings. They both celebrate milestones and are very expensive. However with a wedding there are months of planning complete with rehearsal. Funerals are planned in about 2 hours, and everything is done in one take with no rehearsal. Usually about fifteen minutes before the service, the preacher will show up. Sometimes they will have something printed up to line out what is going to happen. Most often, though, we give them a notepad and they map out the "order of service."

Eighty percent of the time you have the opening remarks, a prayer, a song, the obit, the eulogy, a song, the message, song and then a dismissal prayer. Unless the director is running the music, the main thing we listen for is that dismissal prayer. In the 70's and 80's, every funeral home had an organ, and all the songs were played on the organ. Occasionally, we would have a family request a vocalist as well.

Cassettes came along, but they were hard to que up and could easily break or jam. CD's revolutionized funerals by allowing a more personalized song choice, and these days YouTube means the sky is the limit as far as what you can play at a funeral.

Back in Columbia one afternoon, I was given the order of service. I got distracted, but I knew I had heard at least 2 songs. About 30 minutes in, the preacher started praying. I opened the back doors to the chapel and had Mike dismiss the guests. They were to follow me up to the casket and on out the door. When I got to the casket with about 10 people behind me, the preacher whispered, "I'm not done yet." I glanced behind me at the line of guests pushing forward and whispered back, "You are now." He stood back and just like old pharaoh, he let his people go. I received no complaints. I feel that most folks will hold still for 30-40 minutes tops, but anything longer than that, you not only risk losing their attention but alienate them as well.

Oh. Another good idea is vetting the music you are going to play. Some live versions of rock songs include extremely foul language. You don't want to drop an F Bomb on the crowd. Even old standbys like Tennessee Ernie Ford can get you in trouble. I had a family that requested a certain song, but the only version we had was Ford's.

His rich baritone-bass is soothing. He was crooning away when in mid hymn, he loudly announced, "NOW LET'S EVERYBODY SING!" I hunkered down in the music room and hoped the crowd didn't take his advice. Final piece of advice is cue up the right song. Vince Gill's "Go Rest High" is a very popular choice. That particular CD also contains "What The Cowgirls Do." Pay attention and play track 11 and not track 10. Just saying...BTW..LOL

Funeral Haze

Messing with the new guy is a time-honored tradition in most jobs and in any field. The funeral business is no different in that respect or lack of respect. One of the pet peeves of working a visitation is having someone call and want to talk to a family member. Especially if there is a large crowd there. You have to pick your way through the crowd and then try to identify the requested family member and then pull them away from the folks who cared enough to pay their respects in person.

This particular evening Greg, the new kid, was working. Knowing that young pup wasn't even born yet when "Green Acres" was on TV, I hatched the perfect plan. In my best grizzled old man voice, I called the funeral home and asked to speak to Arnold Ziffel. Anyone over 60 knows that Arnold Ziffel is the pig on Green Acres. I waited patiently for 5 minutes as Greg waded through the crowd trying to find Arnold Ziffel.

At another funeral home, we had a Mr. Bittle in state. I called the funeral home this time as a hillbilly. "Do y'all have Peanut?" The night attendant said, "What?" I repeated, "Do y'all have Peanut? Is Peanut laid out there?" The attendant replied, "Well, ma'am, we have a Mr. James Bittle in state tonight." I finished it with, "Did he go by Peanut? We always called him Peanut Bittle." The kid hung up on me.

My latest stunt was more bold and daring because of the feisty, little gal that handled the visitations in Arkansas. I drove by the funeral home one evening and noticed the parking lot full and cars parked well out into the cemetery. I had never seen such a crowd. I immediately called the funeral home and "Jerrie" answered. Jerrie should have been a school teacher. She was about 5 foot nothing and didn't suffer fools or foolishness. I put on my best confused old man voice and queried, "Uh yes. I was driving by the funeral parlor and noticed the big crowd of folks out there. Could you tell me please who is laid out there tonight?" Jerrie sighed and said, "Mr. Smith." Then I pressed my luck. "Hmmmm. Mr. Smith. Hmmmm. Uh, well, do I know him?" Jerrie abruptly said, "Don Lee, we are too busy for this nonsense!" And hung up the phone. Some people can't take a joke. In her defense, she was as busy as a one-legged man in a behind-kicking contest and really didn't have time for that nonsense.

One more and then I will stop. My favorite trick is to call a funeral home. Any funeral home will do. When they answer say, "Yes. Do you have Miss Mains there?" When they say no, ask again, "Is Myra there?" Then the clincher. "Do you have Myra Mains? Is my remains there!" I kill me.

The Death Rattle

One night around midnight, "Brock," one of our apprentices, and I received a residential call way out in the boonies. We went as far as we could down one road and then turned and did the same down another road or two. I think we left one county and crossed back into another before we finally reached the gravel road leading to the house. It was a small home, and the deceased was laying on a sofa in the living room. Before we loaded up the body, I asked a few pertinent questions such as the time of death and the circumstances surrounding it. Brock and I listened patiently.

The dead man's partner was very animated in her answers. "Well. He wasn't feeling well and just laid down on the couch. Must have been about 10:30 and I heard that death rattle." I said, "Death rattle?" She then did a show and tell. "You know. The death rattle. YEEEEEEEH."

As she hollered, she raised her hand and shook it as she "rattled." Silly me. I had always thought the death rattle was a change in breathing caused by failing lungs not being able to keep up leading to secretions that caused a gurgling sound. Brock is an Iraq-Iran Army war veteran, so he had seen it all and then some. We just looked at each other as she demonstrated that "death rattle" again. We held it together until we were in the van.

The full moon illuminated the night as we headed back to town. The deer were thick that early morning, and I lost count after awhile. Brock was driving, and he slightly veered at one that crossed in front of us. "I always heard that it is best to hit them head on." Brock is a hoot. That woke me up!

The next day during the arrangement conference, I was privileged to see and hear yet another demonstration of the death rattle. "YEEEEH." You learn something new everyday. Brock is a fine young man. He went on to receive both his funeral director and embalmer's licenses and now practices his craft up in Missouri. Thank you, Brock, for your service!

Preoccupied Sons

A retired owner of one of the trade companies died and his family was due in to make the arrangements.

The last time I had seen him was a month or two before. He arrived at a funeral just about service time. As he was looking for a seat, he grabbed a fellow by the arm and loudly announced, "Hey! Last time I saw you, you were with some blonde! Ha Ha!!" What made it even funnier was the fact that this statement was heard throughout the chapel and his victim's wife was not amused.

Anyway, he died, and the family came in the next day. He had a mostly pre-paid funeral plan with us. By "mostly," I mean that he had made 59 out of the 60 payments. His logic was that if he made the final payment, he would die. I don't know if he was serious about this or joking. Anyway, I was gathering the statistical information when I noticed he had 3 sons. Not that uncommon. What was uncommon was the fact that none of his sons was there at the conference. They had all sent their wives to complete the funeral arrangements for this gentleman.

I asked one daughter where the sons were. "Oh. They were going through his closet looking for important papers and came across his porn stash. The boys told us to go on and were still there when we left this morning." Well, alrighty then. Next question.

When making funeral arrangements, you learn to just go with the flow and move on. Nothing to see here, folks.

Third Time's the Charm

She was sitting in the living room of their modest home when the sounds of gunfire shattered her peaceful evening and turned her life upside down. Mrs. Jones was a pleasant lady in her seventies. Her husband had retired to the bedroom a bit earlier than his customary 9 pm bedtime. She took the opportunity to crochet some more doilies and dishrags.

Afraid to go into the bedroom, she called the police and they in turn called us. The coroner would phone in his report in the morning so we were free to remove Mr. Jones. He didn't leave a note nor did Mrs. Jones want to discuss any motives. Either she was in shock or didn't have a clue as to why.

Dennis and I entered the bedroom and were greeted with the grim scene. Mr. Jones was lying on his back in the bed. He was propped up on a couple of pillows.The German Luger he had used to end his life might have been a souvenir from his WWII days. The Luger had been taken by the police. Suicides are permanent solutions to temporary problems. You name it, we see it. Overdose. Carbon monoxide. Shotgun. Pistol. Hanging.

What intrigued me this time was how many shots this elderly gentleman fired. I don't know if it was poor eyesight, hesitation or nerves, but the first shot had lodged in the wall above the bed. The second shot was buried in the wooden headboard. Shot number 3 took a chunk of his ear. Finally the fourth shot ended the heartbreaking drama that played out in that bedroom while the wife relaxed with her knitting. Shot number 4 went through his temple.I will never know why he took his life or why it took 4 shots to do so.

Of all the deaths that really affect me, I would have to say the death of a child ranks number one. Suicides run a close second. I am not ashamed to say that I am human and have been known to shed a tear or two right along with the family.

I Demand to See the Owner

In the good old days before the Federal Trade Commission muddied the waters, arranging the funeral was much simpler. In fact, when I started at Parker's, there was one price card on each casket. That price included the cost of the funeral and the casket. In the early 1980's the FTC came out with a new Funeral Rule and the birth of the general price list.This onerous list required funeral homes to itemize EVERYTHING. This put the burden on the funeral director to not only get the obituary correct and the death certificate correct but to also spend much more time trying to explain and justify each charge. All of this before we could even get down to the details of the funeral.

I had just received my funeral director's license a couple of months before I ran into my first, and I will use a polite term here, "difficult" family. I used to explain the charges before I showed them caskets and outer burial containers. That way they had a ballpark figure of what they could afford. I was a good director but a very poor salesman. I let families decide what they wanted and didn't push them to overspend.

This particular gentleman was making arrangements for his mother. "What is this non- declinable fee?" He barked. I explained that it was a fancy word for overhead. Utilities, salaries, etc. "What is this 24 hour availability? I don't need that. I ain't gonna call you after hours." I explained that because we had to be prepared 24/7 to respond to death calls, we built in the charge. "150 bucks for staff at the visitation? I can work it

myself!" This nitpicking of the price list went on until we came
to the grave opening charges.
"50O bucks to dig a grave? I can hire a backhoe for $40 bucks
an hour!" I had to tell him the cemetery rules forbade anyone
except cemetery employees from digging in our cemetery.

He got angrier and angrier. "You guys got me by the ...." I
demand to speak to the owner!!!" I was forced to tell him the
truth. "You can't speak to the owner." "Why not?" He bellowed.
"Because the owner is in Hawaii for the next 2 weeks," I replied.
His bright red face turned purple. "HAWAII??? No wonder he
can afford Hawaii the way he is ripping me off!!!" I told him we
would be glad to transport his mother to another funeral home
of his choice.

After a couple of phone calls, he decided to stay with us. Oh
joy. Three more days of him. That arrangement was good for
me, though. It helped me develop a tougher hide. Later on, I
would be glad to learn that he was the exception to the rule.
Almost 40 years later, the worst part of the entire job for me was
the business end.

The Apprentice
One bittersweet thing about working for a funeral home in a
town with a Mortuary Science Program is the fact there is a
steady supply of apprentices. The bittersweet part is you get
good help, get used to them, and then ideally they get their
licenses and are kicked out of the nest to fly on their own.

One such little bird was "Jan." Jan was a little gal but strong. I
was apprehensive the first time we received a residential call
together because I am a big old boy and feared a young, little gal
would do more leaning than lifting. Jan not only helped pack a
large guy out of his bedroom late one night but actually took the
lead pulling the cot backwards in the darkened and uneven lawn
full of toys and other debris. Despite the late hour, she was on
time, professional and great help.

Jan was sweet and gullible. Todd, the manager, used this to his advantage. He was explaining to her that at a military funeral we sometimes have to fold a flag and present it to the family. This is true. Especially if an honor guard is unavailable. He also told her that once the flag was folded, she must "march" in a certain cadence holding the flag in front of her exactly 19 inches. This is not true.

Jan was desperately trying to get it "right." She held the flag too close. She held it out too far. Her marching was too sprightly. Her marching was too slow. Todd imitated a high stepping majorette in a marching band to show Jan exactly how she was expected to march the flag to the family. Jan finally realized she had been pranked when Todd told her to get her knees higher in the air as she marched....oh yeah ....and to salute. Her clue that she had been had was the raucous laughter coming out of Todd and myself.

Jan was a jewel. She proved that women can excel and do an excellent job in what for years was traditionally a male-dominated field. I find many families are more comfortable with a woman's touch.

We also found out that Jan's great fear is spiders. Don't ask me how we discovered that one. Miss you, Jan. You are a good example of why the industry needs more women.

A lot of funeral homes contain an oil painting or a portrait of the founders hanging in the lobby. My favorite welcoming advice to any new apprentice was to warn them not to look at the portraits after midnight. Any calls after midnight just avoid the front lobby and use the back stairs. I enjoyed telling them that the eyes in the portrait would follow them around the room. This is all fun and games until it is YOU walking those deserted halls at 2 AM. I am not saying that I ever got spooked. Or did I ??

Eau de Comp

"Eau de comp" - Don's dictionary defines this as "the perfume of someone a couple or three days past their expiration date." One of the downsides of a job in the funeral industry is decomposition. If not refrigerated or embalmed in a day or two, a human body starts to break down. The results are NOT pleasant.

Of all the fellows I worked with, a gentleman named "Hal" seemed to attract these calls. Death tends to hit pretty suddenly when it comes and usually without warning. Hal and I even helped the coroner retrieve an unfortunate fellow from a hot tub one evening. That call is seared into my memory.

Another time on one sunny, mid-summer morning we received a call out in the county. The smell hit us as we pulled into the driveway. Apparently, the gentleman had been felled by a heart attack in his backyard and laid there for 4 or 5 days until the mailman reported that he hadn't been retrieving his mail.

Hal and I retrieved as much as we could but between the hot August sun, the flies and the maggots, there wasn't much left to "retrieve." The smell of decomposition is something that you never forget. A heavy, rubber-zippered pouch will contain everything solid, but the smell which permeates everything is unstoppable.

The only cure for such advanced decomposition is direct cremation. I was so thankful for Hal. He has driven fire trucks in Chicago and was well up to the task of trying to get this body to a cooler ASAP.

Our first order of business was to lower all windows in the van. We then took to the highway, and I held on for dear life as Hal sped and passed every vehicle on the way back - doing well over 20 miles an hour past the legal limit. We had no fear of a ticket because any law enforcement that might stop us would smell our cargo the minute they stepped out of their car.

The decomp smell gets in your hair and your nostrils, and it saturates clothing. I have diminished smell capacity which is a blessing and a curse. The decomp calls don't bother me. Blessing.
Can't taste my biscuits and gravy. Curse. Need a good partner on a decomp call? Call Hal. Need a bank errand? Hal can be there and back before you can say "Son of a Turkey." "Son of a Turkey" is the roughest curse I ever heard come out of Hal. And the printer deserved that moniker because the printer started it. The printer had heard worse from Todd and even threats to be physically thrown out the second story window. Bottom line, Hal is your man for decomp calls and a pleasure to be around.

Hal has an infectious grin. He is knowledgeable about any subject and even though almost 80 years old, he can rise from a kneeling position without using his hands or any props. I never could do that even at an age when I could have done it. "Don't throw in the towel. Better call Hal."

Sheriff

I had only been at this particular funeral home for a few weeks. Early one Saturday just after sunrise, we received a "police" call or "coroner"
call. It was my first encounter with the affable sheriff. The name and county have been left out intentionally. I don't want to be in a heap of trouble.

We drove out a few miles into the countryside. The dew was heavy that morning as we pulled up to the barn. Sheriff greeted us and led us to the body. The obviously deceased fellow was on his back in the newly-plowed field. He was missing the top half of his head. Sheriff somberly shook his head and said, "This is the first man I have ever had to kill in the line of duty." I looked at him and then at the almost headless body and couldn't help but ask, "What did you use, Sheriff? A Bazooka?"

For those of you who didn't watch "Combat" on TV as a kid or one who hasn't served in the military, a bazooka is an anti-tank rocket launcher. Sheriff just looked at me and grinned and gave me the real details. Guy had a fight with his wife and went out in the field and took his own life. This story makes me nostalgic for the good old days when people did the right thing and took their own life instead of taking out a dozen innocent people first.

I recommend much prayer and counseling, but if you absolutely must commit such an act, start with yourself. This man's ending was very sad, but at least he chose to let his wife and young children live.

Sheriff was at another scene in a rural setting. A man had left a note on the kitchen table and then simply walked out the back door and drowned himself in the farm pond behind the house. I asked Sheriff how someone could intentionally drown himself. His response was golden, "I predict that he just laid down on his stomach and started taking on water."

Another classic involving the sheriff was when we got the call to pick up a man who had taken his life down in his basement wood shop. We got there just in time to see Sheriff scooting some sawdust into the pool of blood with his cowboy boot. He then picked up the shotgun (no gloves), held it up to his face as if checking the sights, then racked it to empty the chamber. Sheriff was a throwback to the good old days, and I miss him and that innocent time in my life.

Oops, I Didn't Do It Again

Brandon the manager and I were dressing a body one morning. I quite accidently let out a little puff of stale air. Brandon took off in the other direction and took on like I had done something hideous. "Hey!" "Sorry man. I had Chinese for dinner last night." His watering eyes told more than his next comment. "It is still with you! Something is bad wrong with you! That reeks!!"

We managed to finish our task, and then he received a residential call. Brandon served as coroner as well as the funeral home manager. He left for the residence, and in a few minutes the funeral home received the call as well. The family decided to use us, so Brandon stayed at the house to assist Dick and me with the removal.

The decedent was resting in a recliner. He was clad in a T shirt and boxers. The widow asked if we would put a pair of jeans on him before we took him into our care. Brandon took one leg, and I took the other. As we lifted the legs, a terrible smell saturated the small bedroom. I was going to politely ignore it, but Brandon was overcome. "Dude !?! Seriously !?! You're gonna do THAT in this poor man's bedroom?!?" I said, "Huh?"

Brandon said, "You ripped another bad one!!!" Now I will proudly claim anything that issues from the depths of my septic system, but this bad smell came from the deceased when we lifted his legs. He must have had Chinese the previous evening, too.

To this day I don't think Brandon and Dick believe me. I can laugh about it now, but this false accusation left a bad taste in my mouth as well as the bad smell in that room....

Big and Tall

I am not ashamed to admit that I am bigger than the average bear. Aging, heredity, a sedentary lifestyle and a fondness for biscuits and gravy all are conspiring to keep me morbidly obese. I have found over the years that you can hide up to 80 extra pounds with smoke and mirrors. Or to be more succinct, I have a two-word bit of advice. Bigger clothes. Does a 2X fit tightly? Buy a 4X. Then get ready for the "How much weight have you lost?" comments to start rolling in.

It is my hypothesis that you can get so large you cannot fit through a standard door, but if your clothing is loose enough, you have nothing to fear from body image bullies. I was forced to wear "husky" clothing as a kid and since I am retired, I can satisfy all of my clothing needs at thrift stores. I just look for the 4X T shirts. I embarrassed Robbie at a doctor visit once when I stepped on the scales, and it registered a svelte 297.
I gleefully and loudly exclaimed, "Yes!! Still under 300 pounds!" My winter JC Penny English Fog knockoff trench coat could also double as a graveside tent if needed. I said all that to say this. You may fit in a normal size casket, and they might even be able to close the lid. But you don't want to appear to be wearing the casket.

My first experience with what the industry calls "oversized" caskets was at Memorial.The lady was over 400 pounds which is not that bad on a scale from 200 to 600 pounds, but this was on a 5 foot 2 inch frame. Funeral homes don't have a Big and Tall Dept. The special order 3X casket came in on a separate truck, and surprisingly the ancient hydraulic lift held as we levitated her into the casket. Our first hurdle was the fact that the casket was too wide for the service elevator. I am talking about a casket roughly the size of a hospital bed. We had to actually roll the casketed body around the building and take her in through the much wider front door. Why didn't we just drive her around? We didn't have 8 pallbearers handy to load her up.

Next challenge was that the cemetery required an outer container. Bottom line - we needed an oversized vault which in turn begs for an oversized grave. And I am talking about 8 pallbearers. Men, men, men, men - Manly men. We need lifters here. No leaners need apply. We are talking weight that will make your babies have babies. Hernia-inducing territory. Of course when everything is larger, the cost of the merchandise inflates proportionately as well. Cremation is a sensible and much more economical solution, but that presents its own challenges. That story is for another day.

Mucous Challenged

Ain't nothing colder than a rural cemetery in early February. The skies that had been threatening all morning had started to spit a mixture of freezing rain and sleet. A small crowd had gathered for the graveside service, and we were just about ready to begin when one more car pulled up. I gave the hold it sign to the preacher and pointed to the skinny little old gal being helped up to the tent by a niece or aide.

By the time they made it to the tent, the little old gal was shivering quite briskly. She had on a light sweater, and it was not keeping up with the chill. I removed my trenchcoat and chivalrously draped it around her shoulders and found her an empty chair.

The service was going well, and I knew the weather was going to cut it short. I was feeling a sense of satisfaction and felt I had done my good deed for the day by lending my coat to the elderly lady. I felt someone staring at me and noticed my helper Mason grinning like a possum. I quizzically looked at him, and he nodded toward where my elderly new friend was sitting.

I had noticed she seemed to need a Kleenex or tissue when I seated her but thought no more about it. I glanced again just in time to see her wiping her nose on the sleeve of MY trench coat. I couldn't meet Mason's eyes again because he was apt to lose it and just burst out laughing. Somehow it just wasn't that funny to me. She would repeat this action at least twice more before the preacher concluded the service with a prayer. I helped the mucous-challenged mourner to her car and gingerly retrieved my coat trying desperately to avoid the snot-stained sleeve.

When everyone had left, Mason helped me stack the folding chairs while we waited for the grave digger. "You might wanna get that fancy coat of yours dry cleaned," he gleefully declared.

As the snot froze on my sleeve, the best I could muster was "Thank you, Captain Obvious!" No good deed goes unpunished.

Chillin' in the Cemetery

Back in the late 80's, I bought a 55 Chevy Pickup that one of the embalmers Brian restored for me. In his off time, he was an awesome body and fender man, and he patiently took the time and his talents to make that thing look brand new. My daddy even cut the boards and fitted the bed of the pickup.

I enjoyed driving that old pickup and would leave it at the funeral home on the nights I took the van home on call. I went to drive it home one day after work, and it cranked hard but started. Next night on call, it wouldn't even crank. I put a new battery in. A week later the old truck wouldn't start at all. I was baffled and discouraged.

Brand-new, old truck - and it was a coin toss as to whether it would start at any given day or time. The next night I was on call, I received a death call about 2:30 AM. As I was pulling into the parking lot, I glanced at my unreliable new old truck. I glanced again. I was not accustomed to seeing anyone living or dead in the cemetery at that time of the night /morning. Sure enough, a live person was in the driver seat of MY beloved pickup. He looked either passed out or asleep. I called the police because even back then you never knew if someone was crazy or drunk or armed or a combination of all three.

A patrol car rolled into the parking lot, and we approached my truck. Apparently this homeless guy just enjoyed crawling into the cab of my truck and playing the local FM country music station while passing the night on my restored genuine imitation black leather-looking, vinyl-covered bench seat. Dude at least had good taste in music. Another plus was that he didn't try to hot wire and steal my ride. He didn't even leave any trash or debris in my truck either. It was a harmless pastime, but I really did not appreciate him running my battery down. There was no harm done, and the police let him go. He was given a warning not to pass his nights in my 55 Chevy pickup, and I was given some good advice to actually lock my truck at night. I guess I thought no one would mess with a vehicle parked in a cemetery late at night. I guess I was wrong. That truck was born the same year as I was, and I wouldn't doubt that it is in much better shape. However, all my parts are original.

Politically Correct

A "euphemism" is a fancy word for using fancy words in place of lesser socially-acceptable words. I always thought that a lot of correct terminology was just common sense. However, you can go too far in trying to soften the blow of death that you tiptoe around it in the guise of politically-correct terminology. Just like putting fake green AstroTurf around the waiting grave to soften the

harsh reality and finality, we are taught to use certain words and phrases that, shall we say, aren't as final and harsh. We never ever say that someone died. Nossir. We say they passed. Or passed away. We don't pick up a body or fetch a corpse. Nossir. We take Mr. Smith into our care. We aren't undertakers. Nossir. We are death care professionals. We don't put the body in the hearse (or hurst as a lot of folks call it). Nossir. We place the casket into the coach.

That is fine and dandy except when you are trying to tell 6 pallbearers to face the coach, and they face you instead of the hearse. I prefer "fancy station wagon," but that is just me.

You don't make a house call. Nossir. You make a residential removal. You don't bury somebody in the graveyard. And you especially don't plant someone in the boneyard. Nossir. You inter someone in the cemetery. You don't dig a grave. Nossir. You open a grave. You don't pick out a coffin. Nossir. You find a suitable casket. You don't head to the morgue. Nossir. You head to the prep room or even more vague "head to the back." You don't pick out a tombstone. Nor buy a headstone. Nossir. You select a marker or monument. You don't hand someone their dad's ashes. Nossir. You release the cremated remains of their loved one to them in a special room set up for the transfer of custody. You get the picture.

One memorable Memorial Day, I was accosted by a lady who obviously hadn't gotten the "delicate terminology" memo. I was working a visitation that afternoon when an elderly lady came to sign the book, or more properly, pay her respects to one of her peers. While she had my attention, she said she had heard the tragic news that a young man had lost his life in an automobile accident that day. I agreed that it was a terrible thing.

Then she got to the point. "Uh, yes. Could you tell me how the corpse was mangled?" She uttered this morbid question as she flashed her dentures in a slight grin. How was the corpse mangled??? Admit it. We all wonder why a casket is closed. But to just haul off and lead with, "How was the corpse mangled?" It shocked even this jaded death care professional. I resisted the urge to make up a hideous and gruesome story that would reveal nothing yet satisfy her curiosity but decided to just end this conversation with, "I don't know."

She wouldn't leave not well enough alone. "I heard he was throwed through the windshield and lost a hand." O.K. I didn't acknowledge that latest statement but just showed her to the parlor of her peer so she could sign the book and mull over more morbid matters.

Lose the Monogram

On most all death calls, we always wrap the deceased in a sheet. Some hospitals will shroud the body in a lightweight, white, zippered pouch. After gently placing the loved one on the cot, the final touch is the cot cover. On more than one occasion, I have had a family member request that we do not cover the face. Once we were told to leave the cover tucked down to the chest because they didn't want the neighbors to realize the fellow had died.

Another lady just couldn't bear to see her mother covered up completely. We always comply with any request. In matters of death and grief, there is no right or wrong answer.

One thing Dennis and I did when we went out on our own was ditch the blue velvet cot cover. You know. Looks kind of like a large Crown Royal sack. We determined that a nice quilt without advertising would show more respect. I would offer this advice to any current death care professionals. Lose the velvet cot cover with your funeral home name emblazoned on it. You are not sponsoring a softball team here.

A quilt is a nice touch. One hundred percent of the families we served loved the quilt. Some even suggested that it was like tucking their beloved mother or father in one last time. Families that call you have already chosen to use you. Placing your brand on the deceased is in very poor taste in my opinion. If you are gonna do that, why not add your phone number as well?

On a much lighter note, during one of my father-in-law's hospitalizations, he was distracted by one of his grandchildren. I stealthily retrieved one of my business cards and slipped it between his big toe and the adjoining one. He noticed it shortly thereafter and asked, "Hey?!? What's the big idea, Sonny?" I told him that it would help expedite things if he took a turn for the worse. He just bowed his head, shut his eyes and gave me his trademark "What is wrong with you?" look. Sure loved Bob. Still do. More later on Bob Dilbeck. The man. The myth. The legend.

Whodunnit

She took her own life. Or did she? A former apprentice has been reading these recollections and reminded me of this call in a previous time and galaxy.

We caught the police call to pick up a lady for transfer to the Medical Examiner's office for an autopsy. She was lying on a sheet of plywood on her lawn. A 38 caliber Smith & Wesson Police special had been retrieved, and she had a gunshot wound to the head. Her hands had already been bagged by the folks processing the scene to contain the evidence and make sure she had fired the gun. I couldn't resist adding my two cents worth to the policemen to "help" them solve this case. "So you guys are leaning toward a diagnosis of suicide, eh?" I asked. They affirmed that they were. I paused for dramatic effect and then gave my brilliant reason why it was impossible for her to have done this to herself. "How could she have pulled the trigger with those bags on her hands?" Physically impossible I would say. At least the apprentice thought it was funny. Tough room. Now before all you haters start to hate, let me assure you there were no family members present. And first responders as well as last responders have to keep a sense of humor handy to keep their own sanity.

Last Act of Love

I had just lost the tie and was fixing to don some jeans when my cell phone went off. Carol, the lady attendant manning the funeral home phone that evening, sounded nervous.

"Don? A gentleman is here and says his wife just passed away." O.K. I asked her where the deceased was located. I figured I would talk to the gentleman and get permission for embalming and set up a time for the arrangement conference. Then I would find out where his wife was and if she was ready to be released into our care.

Carol said, "He says she is in his pickup." I asked where his pickup was. "He pulled it around to the carport of the funeral home." I asked her to please ask the gentleman to stay put, and I would be there in less than 10 minutes. In all my years of funeral work, I had never had a husband deliver the body of his wife to us. We usually go to the residence after the coroner has released her.

I sped to the funeral home and pulled around back. I looked in the bed of his old farm pickup. Nothing back there but a spare tire and some baling wire and an odd tool or two. The gentleman came out of the funeral home and opened the passenger side door. His wife was slumped over and held in place by her shoulder/lap seat belt. I felt much sorrow as he told me the circumstances of her death. They lived just over the line up in Missouri, and she had been diagnosed with cancer. Taking care of her, he had exhausted all of his savings. When she finally succumbed, he thought he could save some money if he made the removal himself. He lovingly carried her to the truck, strapped her in, and drove her the 40 miles to us. I was forced to call the local police and get the coroners of both counties involved to sort out jurisdiction of who would sign the death certificate. Thankfully, everyone I came in contact with from law enforcement agreed that he had committed no crime. It just hurt my heart to think he felt he had to do this on his own. I called the other fellow on call that evening, and Mason and I carefully placed her on our cot and slowly rolled her into our building. The gentleman was able to come up with enough for her cremation.

We took off the removal charge as well. Other than the headache of trying to establish who was going to sign the death certificate since it involved two separate counties in two states, the call ended well. This gentleman just did what folks did before they had undertakers. In the old days, he probably could have just buried her on his rural property without the benefit of coroners, law enforcement, or death care professionals. Driving his wife to the funeral home was probably the last act of love he could do for her.

In matters of death and grief, you learn not to judge people. You don't learn this stuff in school. Don't know if anyone reading this ever heard of Minnie Pearl, the comedienne of the Grand Ole Opry. I heard her say something years ago that has stuck with me. "Just love people and they will love you back." Works for me.

Polyester Plum Pants

I was the proud owner of a maroon color pair of polyester slacks that, in my opinion, were very stylish and more than that, were very comfy. This was the mid 1990's, and these pants were an awesome addition to my funeral wardrobe when paired with my navy blazer. Throw in my yellow 6 inch wide tie, and I was a living fashion plate. In my opinion. Well, let me tell you. The first Mrs. Lee thought they were hideous. She described them as "plum" color. She hated those "plum pants" with an unreasonable passion. I am sure that Robbie would ban me from wearing them as well if I still had them. But I am getting ahead of myself.

We had a contract with the prison where we would bury indigent inmates for a set fee. The state paid for a minimal casket, no outer container, and a space in the local cemetery. We kept an assortment of clothing from the Salvation Army and, of course, packaged underwear from Walmart.

It took a while, but we eventually received another indigent inmate with no family. Coincidentally, around the same time period, those "hideous plum" pants mysteriously disappeared from my closet never to be seen again. I am not at liberty to say anything further; however, a certain ex-con may or may not be sporting a new-to-him pair of maroon/plum color polyester slacks. What happens in the inmate section of the cemetery stays in the inmate section of the cemetery.

Kung Fu Funeral

Everything was set up perfectly. All the rolling stock was washed - from the family limo and hearse to the pallbearer limo and flower van. Everything we could control was under control. Wait a minute. Where did those nasty clouds come from?

In the days before color weather Doppler radar when you could see the ominous thunderstorms approaching live in real time on your cell phone, we relied on a forecast given on TV or radio the morning before. "Ten percent chance of rain with highs in the mid eighties." A six-hour-old and rather vague forecast is better than no forecast at all, I guess.

At the start of this particular funeral, the sun was shining and all was well. Sometime between the opening prayer and the third song, a nasty-looking cloud engulfed the skies. Just to be ahead of any problem, we went looking for those huge umbrellas that all funeral homes carry. You know. Those ones that are large enough for a director to hold and still shelter a widow and 2 or 3 other folks.

Anyway, I looked in the storage room,flower room, a couple of closets and down by the wash bay. No umbrellas. The service was winding down when Dennis remembered that the owner had used them the previous day for some kind of charity event. He was out of town today. By the time Dennis had this revelation, it was pouring down rain. We ran downstairs to the owner's office and pulled on the door. "It's locked!" I was going to give up and let the rain have its way, but Dennis had another idea.

He spun around faster than you can say Bruce Lee and went full Kung Fu on that door. He kicked it open and splintered the door jamb in the process. We retrieved the errant umbrellas and raced upstairs in time to escort the family into the limo.
We knew the boss man was gonna be upset upon his return but figured he would rather repair the door than inconvenience and drench the family. One of our goals in funeral service is to help mitigate a family's suffering and not add to it by causing preventable blunders.

The next day the owner saw our handiwork before we could fess up. He admitted that he was upset and livid until he found out the reason for the vandalism.

"I saw that some (expletive deleted) deviate had kicked in my door. First thing that ran through my mind was that one of you (expletive plural deleted again) was trying to steal my giant bottle of scotch." He had an obnoxiously large bottle of J & B in his office. That thing has its own wooden cradle and could probably hold a couple gallons. Once he determined that his liquor was safe and heard the reason behind the violent office invasion, he calmed down. The door jamb was repaired, and the umbrellas were returned to their new home - a five gallon bucket in a corner of the flower room. We also ordered another set of those giant umbrellas to keep in the trunks of the limos. The Morton salt gal ain't got nothing on us. We got you covered. Dennis's mastery of the martial arts came in handy that day.

Dual-Purpose Dentures

Distractions at a funeral can cause a family added grief on top of the raw grief they are already experiencing. Hint. If you must bring a loaded cell phone to a funeral, at least hit the end button before it whistles the entire Andy Griffith theme song at full blast.

Another tip. If you must enjoy the complete song, at least have the common courtesy to not actually answer the call with a loud "VELMA? YEAH. WELL, I REALLY CAN'T TALK LONG BECAUSE I AM AT A FUNERAL."

Another distraction is children running amok and crying babies. It wasn't my pleasure to witness this debacle I am about to recall, but let's just say it is from a reliable source.

Imagine a small country church packed wall to wall with standing room only. Which in all honesty in this church is about 75 people. Imagine, if you will, a young mother - and I am talking mid to late teens here. She had a baby in her arms and a toddler clinging to one hand and another with a death grip on her leg. The baby was ok because she had a "binkie," or pacifier, holding her attention. One toddler was distracted with another toy. This left the other toddler with nothing to do but holler and whine.

My reliable source almost had to turn away from the sight he witnessed. If you have a weak stomach, you read on at your own risk of vomiting. The teenage mother reached into her mouth and pulled out her dentures. She gave them to the toddler as a substitute pacifier. Once the child started sucking on them, all was well again. You were warned. Teen mom with dentures. And what if those dentures had been someplace unsanitary like the floor or something?

But bless her heart she silenced her kids in respect of the occasion. Long story short. Control your cell phone and keep an extra pacifier or two handy at the next funeral you are compelled to attend.

Full Moon Friday

It was Friday afternoon about a quarter to five, and I was walking to the funeral home from the front parking lot for my 5 pm shift. The curtains were open in the large floor-to-ceiling window in the front office. I glanced at the office and then looked again. A double take. Yeah. That's what I did.

One of the embalmers, Mark, had dropped his pants and was shaking his bare behind at me. Well, actually at me and whoever was driving by on the Business Loop. This was during the height of the mooning craze. I entered the front door, and we both had a good chuckle about his lowbrow attempt at humor. While it was not exactly horseplay nor hijinks it was probably not a good idea just on general principle. If we would have had an employee handbook or a Human Resources Dept., mooning would probably have been a written notice no no. But most men never advance out of junior high in their mentality of what they think is funny. In fact I am 64 years old and still find his action funny.Ha Ha funny.

Anyway I had just made it to the cemetery office downstairs when the funeral home line lit up. I answered it and the caller did not have a question nor need our services. They simply offered a little sarcastic advice. "This is Wilkerson's Nursery. Do you have any sunglasses over there?" I wondered why the plant and tree nursery across the street from the funeral home would make such an odd request."Huh?" Then came the kicker. "We noticed that the moon is shining pretty bright over there. You might need some sunglasses." Well, I guess my lack of response to this sarcastic barb didn't sit well, so they took it up a notch and called the owner at home. The next phone call came from the owner. At home."Which one of you (expletive deleted) deviates mooned Wilkersons??" I listened to him vent until his anger subsided and promised it would never happen again. And it didn't.Until the next time.

Bad Smell on 8th Floor

Penguin Towers. Fifteen stories of government subsidized housing. Tallest building in town. It was a bad smell that brought us here on this nasty, cold and rainy evening. Apparently, Dennis and I were needed at Apt. 905. If you happen to be living in the Towers these days, I will ease your mind. The good news is I just pulled Apt 905 out of my head as an example. The bad news is that you may or may not be living in the actual apartment now.

Our first hurdle was remembering which elevator was long enough to accommodate our cot. Well, actually you could cram the empty cot in one of the lifts but when loaded, it had to go in the one on the right. We reached the 9th floor, and the smell engulfed us as we exited the elevator. Funny thing about an unattended death is that it is like a puppy needing a potty break. First a friendly "woof." Then an anguished whine. Eventually, an angry bark that intensifies until you let him out or pay the consequences. Same with an undiscovered body. No problem for a day or two, but if ignored, that mild odor turns into a stout stench that, left to its own devices, will eventually turn into a funk typhoon. In other words, he was found because after 5 days he made his presence known to anyone walking the halls of the 9th floor. We followed our nose (it always knows) to #905.

The door was slightly ajar, but we knocked anyway. A muffed "Come on in" gained us entrance. Besides the stench, we were greeted by the unfortunate officer who drew the short straw that night. He was spraying "Stench Be Gone"
with one hand and holding his nose with the other.

Those apartments are all the same. A bedroom/living room, tiny kitchen and a bathroom. Dennis and I glanced hopefully at the bed, but it was empty. The officer removed his hand from his nose, shook his head and pointed us to the bathroom while still applying the Lysol spray. We headed to the bathroom and were greeted with a macabre sight. Now when an undertaker uses a fancy word like "macabre," take my word. It was macabre. And hideous.

The fellow had found an unusual way to kill himself. He was hanging by the neck from coaxial cable tied to the shower head. He had a bandana- type handkerchief covering the lower part of his face tied on like he was fixing to rob an 1880's era bank or stagecoach. The kicker was the gallon milk jugs of water tied to his feet to help weigh him down so he could hasten the asphyxiation process.

Coming in a close second to the hideous sight was the hideous smell. Well, one of us cut him down while the other held him steady so he would slump into the body bag. It was highly unusual to have this intense odor without the flies and their ugly cousins, the maggots.

We got him loaded and took him to the hospital morgue to await his autopsy to make sure he rigged his death himself.

Epilogue: Late the next afternoon after his autopsy, the hilarious but gruff diener (the person who makes the rough cuts for the Medical Examiner) told me to "Get that stinkin' (expletive epithet that implies an Oedipal relationship) out of here!!!" Well, besides the cursing, he did have a point. Would you want that guest in YOUR office any longer than necessary? His next stop was the crematory. He has since become just another "misty water-colored memory." A dead time story filed away in the dark corners of my mind.

Dead or Asleep?

Most nursing homes usually have 2 folks confined to a room. Each occupant usually has their own dresser and hospital bed.

My first solo nursing home call happened about 10 pm. Most of the inhabitants had been asleep for awhile by the time I made it to the darkened room. So far so good. The temporary name placard by the door read John Smith and Bob Jones. I was there after Mr. Smith and crept quietly into the room not wishing to wake Mr. Jones. It was my first solo call, and I wanted to be a success in my new career. O.K. I saw two elderly gentlemen in separate beds. Both were lying flat on their backs in the supine position. Both heads were tilted back. Both men had their eyes closed and mouths agape. Trouble is that one man was dead and the other was asleep.

It was not my pleasure to know Mr. Smith and besides,the semi darkness only made their similarities well, more similar. I thought a round of eeny, meeny, miney, moe would be rather gauche and or inappropriate. I was forced to make a judgement call and committed myself to bed number 2. I was just fixing to grab his draw sheet to pull him onto my cot when Mr. Jones opened his eyes and gave me a look that said, "Well, what is it this time? BP check? Forget my horse pill?" I bowed awkwardly and murmured an apology as I backed up and pulled his curtain closed. Thankfully, I heard his steady breathing turn into a snore as I approached the bed of his roomie. This gentleman cooperated and allowed me to take him into my custody without any further miscues. I sure hope I grabbed the right dentures.

Bob Dilbeck

I asked him for permission to marry his daughter. He glanced away from the Weather Channel. "Do you think you can take care of her?" I said, "Yes!" He said, "OK" and then returned his attention to the TV. Bob, or Bobby, became the closest thing to a dad to me since my own father had died. I was fortunate to have 2 awesome dads in my lifetime. Bob became not only my mentor but a genuine hoot to be around.

As Jaci grew, he said, "It's a good thing she's adopted because you two couldn't produce something that good looking." Bob spoke out of both ends quite fluently. He always blamed any new ailment on his "aorta." His aorta had ruptured in his 60's, and he lived in spite of overwhelming odds. Bob made the two-day trip to see the Grand Canyon only to sit in the car and not even look out the window. Bob showed his behind at least 3 or 4 times a week, but it was due to the loose khakis that he favored.

Bob told us he was dying. In the hospital that last Christmas Day he rebuked his son for praying for his recovery. "I am trying to D Y E and Doug won't let me." Just after New Year's Day we found out he had incurable cancer. After the doctor broke the news to Bob, I went to his bedside to see how he was handling such a blow. He looked me in the eye and said, "Well, I guess you can have your riding lawn mower back. I won't need it."

The doctor gave him something to help him breathe, and then surrounded by loving family he died. Peacefully. Suddenly. Calmly. Secure in the knowledge of his next address. I cried silently. His wife and daughter cried loudly. Doug was stoic, but you can't hide love when it needs to exit. His tears were flowing as well. Doug's wife was crying. Drake and Calli said goodbye, and we lifted Marlee up so she could kiss him as well. I made a call, and soon a gal from the funeral home I worked at showed up to help me bring Bob back.The embalmer did a good job, and we decided to bury Bob with the blue stone ring he was so proud of. He had always wanted a ring with a blue stone. I hadn't worn my old college ring since the 80's. I gave it to him, and he wore that thing proudly.

The retired manager of the funeral home and the regional manager both worked the service so I could just be family. His earthly remains and a good chunk of our hearts lie in a beautiful country cemetery across from a pasture filled with cattle. Sleep well, Bob. You sure were good at it here.

How Would You Do It?

A year or so before my entry into funeral service, I had a discussion with Barry. Barry was a fellow that helped my uncle at the welding shop. It was a summer job for me, and we killed the time between fixing broken farm implements and installing trailer hitches with idle chatter about anything and everything. Somehow the topic of suicide came up. I told him I would never consider it. He pressed the issue until I gave him a theoretical method of preference. "I think I would just pull the truck in the garage, put in my favorite 8 track tape, put the door down and leave it running until I or the truck ran out of gas."

Barry halfway listened as he flipped the welding helmet down and laid a bead across a piece of channel iron. Fast forward a couple of years. I was now a newbie at Parker's.

The guys were backing the hearse down the alley and I watched as they unloaded a body and rolled it into the prep room.

Being a native of the town, I asked who they had picked up. "Some guy named Barry. Barry Smith." I had a sick feeling in the pit of my stomach. "What happened to Barry?" I did but really didn't want to know. "He killed himself. Carbon monoxide. Had a half empty bottle of Jack Daniels in the cab of his truck with him." Nowadays you can find even easier ways to end yourself - what with the internet and what not. My urgent plea is this. Don't. Please get help. Call a friend. Reach out. Someone always cares. Pray. Take your problems to God. There is enough natural death to go around. We can wait.

Tu Tu Much Information

Please don't ask me how it got started. It was a slow week at the funeral home. This was around 1984, and I was still young enough and dumb enough to try anything once. The cemetery secretary dared me to wear a tutu. Knowing full well that they didn't make one my size, I took the dare. She then revealed that she was quite the seamstress, and she could actually MAKE me a tutu.

The morning of my debut arrived. I quickly donned my gay apparel complete with a stunning tiara. I may be a bit prejudiced, but I would say my legs are my best feature. At least they were. Back before my knees started leaking hydraulic fluid. Anyway, part of the dare involved getting into the waiting 6 door limo. There happened to be some roofers working on the new addition, and I couldn't help but notice the sound of hammers not hammering. "Mark" held the limo door open for me, and with all the diva attitude I could muster, I demurely climbed into the back seat. We took a couple of slow circles around the cemetery then returned. I exited the limo proudly. I ignored the catcalls from the roofers and kept my head high as I executed a pirouette and ballerinaed back into the funeral home. I am so glad that this was before cell phone videos and social media. However. Anyone that purchases the print edition of my book will be able to see the sole surviving picture taken that day. I will autograph it. For an extra charge, I will even tear that page out and burn it before purchase.

Just A Peek

Personalization of funeral services has evolved exponentially since I came on board in the late 70's.
Back then you had a guest book and maybe a framed photo of the deceased taken 10 years prior by that prolific photographer Olan Mills.

If you wanted songs, they were performed on the house organ and we hired a vocalist if desired.
Later, little programs or folders were introduced with the service details and obituary printed on them as a keepsake for the attendees. Around the time my wife died, we had progressed to a magnetic memory board that would hold about 25 to 30 snapshots and we played our music on CD's.

Eventually by the time I migrated down to Arkansas, we were able to produce video DVD's of pictures brought in by family members and even downloaded off their cell phones. A gentleman had died, and his wife brought in the obligatory 35 photos for the video. She picked out a song to be played while the pictures fade in and out and a theme for the video. The pictures were scanned and then sent to our production company in Dallas where the final product was produced and made available for us to download and make copies. The finished product plays on a continuous loop on a large TV set up in the chapel. It had been playing all afternoon when we drew the complaint from a patron. Apparently one of the photos featured a cookout scene where a few guys were enjoying their Bar-B-Que. The second guy from the right was squatting in a pair of shorts. You had to look pretty hard, but since this picture was blown up to fit a 60 inch TV screen and paused for 30 seconds and zoomed in, you could catch a glimpse of "pouch" that had escaped the confines of his shorts. Now if that ain't personalization, I don't know what is. Our general manager viewed the offensive footage and after 3 "Oh "craps!," he immediately pulled the plug on the video. We then frantically called Dallas to see if they would remove the offending picture and send us the G rated version. By the time the official visitation started, we had the edited version playing. I guess you really can't tell the scope of your photography until it is blown up to a TV size that accommodates the hard of seeing. Here is a tip for you camera buffs and budding photographers: Watch out for photo bombers. Don't let that Kodak moment turn into a Maalox moment.

Why You Wear Red Watch?

"Why you wear red watch?" The Oriental lady across the arrangement conference table must have gotten tired of my questions because she fired off one of her own.

Her husband had died after a lingering illness, and she was trying to supply answers to my questions to fill out the death certificate and obituary. I will admit that before I finally settled on an Apple Watch, I must have owned at least 40 wristwatches over the years.

On this particular day, I was sporting my Arkansas Razorbacks Fossil watch featuring a red dial. This was back a few years ago when they had a respectable football team.

"Why you wear red watch?" I told her I was a Hogs fan. This earned me a look I have seen on my mama's face over the years. A mixture of disapproval and disapproval. As I was walking her to the door at the end of the arrangements, I asked her if I could give her a hug.

Usually I don't ask because hugs are spontaneous signs of empathy and comfort. I have shed tears with families and given and received hugs freely. Because of the watch incident, I thought a hug would break the ice. Maybe an international sign of care and concern. So I asked her, "May I give you a hug?" She recoiled like I had broken wind or stepped on her foot and said, "Maybe later." Well, I don't take rejection kindly and Googled the terms "red" and "Oriental."

Best I can tell, my Razorback watch offended her because the color red in Korea symbolizes passion and is a very inappropriate color for them to wear. It all came together for me. Not only was I wearing an inappropriate sign of passion, I was trying to seal the deal with an amorous hug. I said all that to say this. Go Hogs! And if hugging hurting people is wrong, I don't wanna be right.

Grand Theft Auto

The old 1977 Chrysler Station Wagon with the fake wood siding had seen much better days. In its prime, it had served as a removal vehicle for the Burnett Funeral Home in Ashland, MO. By the time Memorial Funeral Home acquired Burnett's, the old tank was relegated to more mundane tasks such as errands, trips to Columbia and back, and the occasional loan when an employee had a vehicle in the shop. By the late 80's, minivans had replaced station wagons as the go to removal and trip vehicle. The old dog wasn't much to look at, but it had the obnoxiously large 400 cubic inch V-8 motor and was kind of fun to drive. In fact, I got a speeding ticket coming home one night from Ashland after a visitation.

Anyway, it lived out back of the funeral home, and whenever we needed a spare company vehicle, it was as faithful as an old dog. Apparently, we didn't need a spare vehicle for 2 or 3 weeks and didn't even notice the wagon was missing. I guess we all assumed it was parked at the funeral home in Ashland or someone had it out on an errand or road trip. Eventually, the alarm was sounded. "Have you seen the Burnett wagon?" No.

"Has anyone seen the Burnett wagon?" No. "When is the last time you saw the Burnett wagon?" Been awhile.

We hastily decided that some "deviate" had stolen the Burnett wagon and decided to call the Police Department and report the theft of our beloved mascot or mascar. About a week after we reported the Grand Theft Auto, we received a call from the Police. "We found your station wagon. We will meet you where we found it. Bring a key and it's yours." We hurried over to a lot next to an auto repair shop. There sat our prodigal wagon. The policeman said, "You can tell someone has gone through the glovebox and made a mess all over the entire interior." I looked into the wagon and had to grin. "Uh sir. That is how we left it. That car gets rode hard and put away wet. It always looks disheveled." Case solved. No one had stolen the car.
One of the embalmers had driven it to the auto Repair shop to pick up his pickup and left it there.
We didn't even miss it until we missed it. The wagon felt like a long lost friend as I slipped behind the wheel and drove it back to the cemetery parking lot. It might even still be there. Or not. Who would know?

On a Hill Far Away

A lot of country cemeteries are set up on a hillside. I don't know if it is for enhanced drainage or simply the view, but some can be quite steep.
I was tickled to see that the tent was set up over the grave. Sometimes catching a glimpse of the green or blue tent helps a director to find the cemetery before he or she drives past it.

An elderly gentleman had lost his wife, and his son insisted on pushing his dad's wheelchair up the hill to the graveside for the brief service. The service was non-eventful, and I wanted to make sure that old boy made it safely back to his son's car. We decided to turn the wheelchair around and back it down the hill. We didn't need any runaway wheelchairs or any other preventable accidents especially after everything else had gone so well.

I faced the widower in the chair, and his son started backing him down the incline. They hit a slight imperfection in the ground or a gopher hole or something, and one of his feet slipped off the foot rest. The son kept backing, and I reached down to place the old fellow's foot back on the metal rest plate. I was baffled and mesmerized as his leg started to grow longer right before my eyes. That thing must have lengthened by 12 to 18 inches. The further the son backed, the longer his daddy's leg grew.

Finally, it slipped completely out of his pant leg and hit the ground. It sure was a nice-looking prosthetic, complete with nice black dress sock and polished black Oxford shoe. Well, what do you do? I decided to get a leg up on the situation. The son just told me to hand the leg back to his dad. The elderly gentleman chuckled and said, "Hee hee my leg fell off again!"

I was instructed to just lay it slaunchwise across his lap for the rest of the trip back to his car. We got his dad tucked back into his son's car and put the errant leg into the backseat. After loading up the wheelchair, I ascended the hill again to wait for the casket to be lowered. Everyone took the lost leg incident in stride. Just another day at the cemetery.

Oh Tannenbaum

Memorial Funeral Home had a tradition of a small tasteful Christmas tree being set up a week or two after Thanksgiving in the corner of the lobby. Kind of opposite and to the left of the fireplace. That was back in the days when you anticipated the season instead of getting burned out by Thanksgiving by all the hype promoting the overspending starting before Halloween.

Some families found comfort in the paradox of pretty lights warmly shining in a place of cold, dim sadness. This particular year the office manager, "Sara Fay" produced a company check and commissioned "Chet" to procure the tree. The first volley in the Battle of Tannenbaum was fired when Chet came back with a hideous flocked tree. By flocked I mean someone had sprayed it with fake snow that flaked off all over the carpet and filled its designated corner of the funeral home lobby and then some. Sara Fay wasn't happy with this whitewashed freak fir masquerading as a Christmas tree. Nor was she happy with the rather large and tacky ornamental balls Chet had chosen to adorn the tree with. She let that slide because she could simply replace them with some more suitable ornaments she had squirreled away from past celebrations.

So far the score was 1 to 1. Sara Fay conceded defeat on the tree choice, and Chet backed down on the ornaments. The final battle came with the tree topper. Chet had picked up a rather jolly-looking Santa Claus to place on top of the tree. Sara Fay held her tongue, but her face betrayed her feelings. The very next morning when Chet came in he gave a sideways glance at the tree. "HEY!! WHERE'S MY SANTIE??" He angrily bellowed. In place of his "Santie" was an equally hideous angel. The somewhat childish battle of the tree topper went back and forth a couple of days. One morning, old Santa would be perched on top of the tree and the next morning the angel would be topping the flocked fir.

The battle finally ended in a compromise when someone produced a star that both parties could agree on. The star reigned supreme over the albino fir that year. I think the next year they bought a flockless artificial pre-decorated tree. A bit of advice. Prepare for the flak if you go for the flock.

Chet has gone on to own a funeral home of his own. You can't miss it. Every year in December he has a life size "Santie" in a sled pulled by eight plastic reindeer perched on the roof of his funeral home. "Feliz Navidead." Or as Sara Fay would probably say, it is a prime example of a "Feliz Navidon't."

Convenient Downtown Location

Part of the charm of my first job in funeral service was the location of the business. Parker's had been in business since the 1880's. It was located downtown in the old business district. The upstairs had been a furniture store, and the downstairs had once been an automobile dealership. The current incarnation included an apartment upstairs. I was too young to appreciate the history of the old building. To me, it was just a cool place to work. A favorite pastime at visitations was just watching the activity on the sidewalk out front from the glass panels at the top of the doors. We had a "regular" named "Step and a Half" who worked nearby. He would limp by us while Greg would open the door and invite him in with a crooked finger.

"Hey?!? What's your hurry? Come in. Stay awhile! Stay!!" The guy would just shake his head and limp a little faster out of our radar. He must have enjoyed this morbid banter because he came by everyday for his greeting. My favorite times at the door were watching an elderly patron trying to parallel park their boat-sized Buick. A lesser man would drive on into the parking garage or let their grandkid take them to the visitation or take a taxi. Not this blue hair. Nossir.

OK Let's get her lined up. Good good. Now put her in reverse and cut the wheels to the right. Oops. That was left. OK. Reverse and crank it right. Good, good, good BAM!!! Hit the bumper of the car behind her. OK. Now put her in drive and crank the steering wheel left or right. Good good BAM !! Hit the car in front of her. Repeat this action a couple of times until wedged in parking space.

Some of those folks could make an entire career out of one parking attempt. Not trying to shame old folks or limpers here because I have joined the ranks. Part of the reason I felt at home there was I remembered vividly when we had my grandmother laid out there in 1964. I had a couple of uncles laid out there during my tenure as well. The other reason I loved my years there was because it was like a living situation comedy. I hear that the building is gone now. Another victim of downtown condo development. At the risk of sounding like an old retired man, I must say that the people and times were much more innocent 40 years ago. I am fortunate that I have so many good memories of my working years.

Creutzfeldt Jacob Disease

Creutzfeldt Jakob Disease. Perhaps you have heard of this. Maybe you have heard of Mad Cow Disease. Same thing. It is a degenerative brain disease that usually leads to certain death within 6 to 9 months of diagnosis. Back when I came in contact with it in 1985, pretty much all they knew about this disease is that it was highly contagious and 100 percent fatal.

It was a typical nursing home call, and I am pretty sure that early in my career, I wasn't wearing gloves when I took Mrs. Jones into my care. This was years before universal precautions and gloves were recommended but not mandated. And it was light years before folks were covered head to toe in astronaut-looking space suits for such a call.
No one at the nursing home thought it important enough to mention to me the cause of her death.

During the embalming, we received an afterthought call to "warn" us about her
condition. We were advised that something called "prions" were an indestructible part of this disease, and it was advised to bury any embalming instruments used in her procedure with her. I called the medical examiner who was a renowned forensic pathologist and asked him the symptoms of this horrible and fatal disease.

He gave a list: amnesia, delusion, dementia, disorientation, inability to speak or understand language, lack of concentration, or mental confusion, jerking muscle spasms, overactive reflexes, problems with coordination, rhythmic muscle contractions, or slow bodily movement, anxiety or apathy, depression or hallucination, blurred vision, difficulty speaking, insomnia, personality change, or rapid involuntary eye movement. I was feeling paranoid enough, but when he gave me the sorry news that CJD can lie dormant for up to 15 years before it manifests itself, I felt even worse. After the symptoms manifest themselves, you die within 6 months.

I have almost made it 20 years past the 15 year mark, but this call was always in the back of my mind. For years I kept a Xerox copy of the death certificate with the CJD cause of death in case my widow needed the money. I figured an opportunistic law firm could at least get my final expenses paid for. The other more important lesson I learned was to wear gloves on ALL calls for my own protection. Universal precautions.Treat everybody and every body like they are contagious.

Cemetery Crew

Cemeteries are an integral part of the death care business. I have had the privilege to work at a couple of funeral homes with attached cemeteries.

Back in the 80's the grounds crew consisted of a couple of brothers. I guess we should have known one of them had a serious alcohol problem when he punched the owner of the funeral home at the company Christmas party. It wasn't a dramatic fight like you see at the end of every Lifetime movie. Just a tap really. But enough to foreshadow the incident that got him relieved of his job.

Later that winter, "Dale" wasn't at work by 8. Nor by 9. His brother showed up to convey the sad news that Dale had gotten a DWI that morning. Yes. That morning. On his way TO work. DWI's are pretty much job killers at any time, but how early do you have to start drinking to get one on your way TO work?

When we finally got a good crew together, "Edgar," the cemetery superintendent or cemetery sexton started displaying early signs of dementia. The first clue that all was not well was the day he was mowing and got too close to the assembled VFW honor guard getting ready for a funeral. They hadn't had that close a call since their overseas days in WWII. You don't expect to be strafed by friendly fire in the Veteran section of the cemetery.

Another section of the cemetery contains a small goldfish pond. We always called it the "Cement Pond." The news spread quickly the day he drove his Heckendorn 88" cut mower into the cement pond. That stunt pretty much grounded Edgar, but he still hung around to give advice and keep his finger on the pulse of the cemetery.

Another feature of that cemetery is the mausoleums. Before the owners paid the money for an expensive, yet much safer, mechanical lift, we had a rather clumsy and dangerous scaffolding structure to elevate the casket into the upper crypts. One false move and someone calls the Hurt Line and tells them they mean business.

I can see the commercial: "Have you been crushed by a falling casket?" "Has someone else's death almost led to your death?" The scaffolding idea was retired the day we were driving by the mausoleum and saw "Pete" hanging by one foot about 10 feet off the ground and hollering "HELP"!! Here's to the unsung heroes of funeral land. The cemetery boys. You guys are over worked, underpaid, and under appreciated. You are crucial in making the guys in the suits look good at their jobs. Salute!

Blindsided

Closing the casket seems to be the hardest part for a mourning family to bear. Something about hearing the latch catch or watching the lid descend just puts a stamp of finality on the proceedings.

Some folks decide to just leave the casket open for the entire service and then have us close it when they have said their final goodbyes and are out of sight and safely in the limo. Other folks prefer we just leave the casket closed for the service and not reopen it. It really is just a family preference that we try to accommodate.

One of the funeral homes I worked at had a nice family room off to the side of the chapel. It had vertical blinds that could be drawn shut at any time during the service.

On this particular day "Darryl" had seated the family and had drawn the blinds closed so they wouldn't have to endure the sight of him closing the casket. He lifted the casket spray of flowers while Mark gently closed the lid. He then walked to the side and exited past the organist. The rather lengthy service went well, and it came time to dismiss the assembled guests. A couple of guys dismissed them, and when Darryl went to release the family, he immediately noticed something wrong.

The family was rather quiet. Quieter than usual and had a look of distress. More distressed than usual. Darryl asked them the dreaded question. "Is something wrong?" "It sure would have been nice if we could have seen the funeral." Darryl had forgotten to pull the blinds open after he closed the casket. The family had sat the entire 45 minutes in a darkened room with no view. Ouch.

I am sure Darryl was as embarrassed as much as the family was upset. His failure had blindsided both him and the family. Darryl was forgiven, and if that's the worst mistake he ever made in his funeral career, I envy him.

Handicapped Parking

Funeral director conventions, especially in the 80's, gave hometown undertakers a chance to go to another town and let off some steam by consuming much alcohol and bragging (usually lies) about how much business they were generating. I actually felt sorry for some of the vendors.

I didn't witness this particular incident but heard it from my reliable and confidential source.

A well-known burial vault company sponsored a nice buffet one evening; while the gentleman from the vault company was giving a couple of opening remarks, a few drunken undertakers could be seen ignoring their host and heading straight for the chow line.

Ted was a salesman for a steel burial vault company, and he and 3 or 4 undertakers commandeered a 6-door limo from David, owner of a funeral home near the Lake of the Ozarks. After assigning a designated driver, they headed out and decided to make a quick stop at a liquor store for a couple cases of beer. They pulled the limo into a handicapped space and entered the store. Ted put the beer on the counter and David started to pay.

The young girl behind the counter had given them the stink eye when they entered the store and could barely contain her anger now. David asked her, "Do you have a problem, Miss?" She did have a problem and unloaded on David. "You guys make me sick!! Pulling into a handicapped space in your big fancy car. Those spaces are for handicapped people!!!"

David simply lifted his pant leg and removed his prosthetic left leg and THUMPED it HARD down on the counter. "Is that handicapped enough for you??" He then put his leg over his shoulder and hopped out the door on one leg. "Ted? Grab the beer!" Ted finished paying for the beer and followed David back out to the limo. You just never know who or what is lurking under that Joseph A. Bank suit and tie.

More Chet Shenanigans

Craig, our student employee, lived above the funeral home. He preferred to do his cleaning chores early in the morning before class at the University. Chet knew Craig's schedule very well. Their paths crossed early one morning.

Chet was at the funeral home around 5 AM and had just finished embalming when he set his trap. He snuck into the chapel and laid down between a couple of pews. It didn't take long until he heard Craig working his way towards him with the vacuum. He was just about to Chet's pew when Chet stealthily grabbed Craig's ankle in an icy death grip.

According to Chet and with verification from Craig, it appears that Craig let out a squeal that could be heard by dogs a mile away and then proceeded to climb up the wall backwards to escape whatever demon that had tried to pull him down.

Our student help really deserved combat pay for putting up with Chet. Chet also enjoyed scaring floral delivery folks by suddenly appearing behind them as they passed by the music room with their hands full of peace lilies or the large fragile pom pom mums that would shatter and disintegrate if you just looked at them the wrong way. Our favorite victim we had dubbed "Wings" because of the teleflora ballcap he always favored, featuring Mercury wings.

Chet loved to grab Wings from behind and let out a cross between a rebel yell and banshee scream.
It got so bad that Wings would always fearfully and carefully look around before approaching the flower room.

Chet drove an AMC Pacer. It was an odd-looking widetrack glassy, little car that never really caught on but seemed to suit Chet's personality.

Chet took a liking to Runts candy. They are basically a chunk of hardened sugar molded into fruit shapes such as banana, cherry, lime and orange. Good stuff but hard to find at the time. Chet was out on errands one day and stopped at a Quick Sack. He asked the little gal behind the counter, "Excuse me, miss. Do you have the Runts?" She looked baffled."Pardon me? What did you say?" Chet again made his request. "The Runts. I said, 'do you have the Runts?' " Why was this man asking her if she had diarrhea? Finally, with the help of his interpreter (me), they determined that the store did not carry them. Chet was a barrel of laughs crammed into a 55 gallon drum.

To View the Unviewable

Fatal farming accidents, while relatively rare, actually happen more often than you would think. They usually involve a tractor or grain elevator. I have even made a removal from a hog lot, but the victim had succumbed to a heart attack and just happened to die where he fell.
** Extreme morbid warning! Read the next part after breakfast!**

And, yes. A hog will eat human flesh. Enough said. Before you get too smug and say, "Glad I don't own a hog," you need to realize that if you die unattended and that cute little lap dog or sweet old cat gets hungry before you are discovered you need not worry. They will get fed. They tend to go for the easy-to-reach and soft parts like the face, nose and ears first. Just leave the toilet lid up and they are set.

But I digress. Back to our story. Farming accidents can be gory, but if the damages are from the neck down, it is always 100 percent viewable.

Our story today involves a farmer whose tractor overturned on him and dealt him a crushing injury to the right side of his face. Now for those of you who notice these things, it is the right side of the face you see when the body is laid out in the casket. In our neck of the woods, we use what they call a half-couch casket. Only the top half is opened up. Whereas Count Dracula on the other hand usually uses a full-couch coffin. The entire body is viewed as if the lid is one piece.

The damages to this farmer were too devastating to be repaired.The right side of his face had severe crushing injuries while the left side was relatively unscathed. He could be made to look human but not close enough to look like this particular human.

Kind of like when President Kennedy was assassinated, and they had the best embalmers money could buy. The embalmers worked their magic all night long. When Jackie viewed the results her comments were, "It's not Jack." In other words he looked like someone. Just not President Kennedy.

This particular young widow desperately wanted an open casket because of the number of relatives this man had. Dennis came up with a brilliant idea. I have never seen this done before or since. He said, "Why don't we put him in the casket backwards. Turn him around where the left side of his face is on view. Open the foot panel instead of the head panel and throw a ball cap on him."

Now the interior of the foot panel of a casket is not nearly as pretty as the head panel. It doesn't have the fancy velvet or crepe interior but does have a passable white cardboard lining. We presented the gentleman in the unorthodox manner, and his wife and kids were so grateful they could see him. They even opted to leave the foot panel open for the viewing and funeral. Dennis and I could tell that some of the guests could tell that something wasn't quite right, but unless you see casketed bodies day in and day out, it wasn't that noticeable. If any current death care professionals are reading this, please feel free to employ this technique on your next problematic case.

Nothing to See Here, Folks

One Sunday afternoon a month, a few church members and myself would gather at a local nursing home and sing a few hymns, give some encouragement, give a brief Bible lesson and pray for the residents. The residents seemed to enjoy the service, and we always felt a little better our own selves after providing a bit of cheer for these folks.

We would gather in a common area in the middle of a hub that served 4 hallways. More often than not, I was on call during these Sunday visits. I always had a cot loaded and ready in the removal van so I could expedite things when needed.

We tried to stick with songs that the residents knew so they might be encouraged to sing along with us. I think we were on the second verse of "Precious Memories" when my pager went off. I slipped out to return the call. An elderly gentleman had expired. No problem. What troubled me was that he had died at the nursing home we were currently singing at. I stepped out into the parking lot and grabbed the cot. I had to roll the empty cot past the assembled residents and singers. AWKWARD. I proceeded to the room and took the decedent into my custody. I then had to roll the now-loaded cot past the still assembled residents and singers. AWKWARD AGAIN. It could have been worse, I guess. The dining area was across from the common area. At least I didn't have to wheel the deceased fellow past the lunch bunch.

MIZ-ZOU

Another football Saturday in Columbia, MO. I was still in training, so I tagged along on a call that usually only required a single person. We had received the call that someone had died at the Medical Center, and the body was ready to be released to us. The Medical Center is connected to the Veterans Hospital by a tunnel that goes under the road between them. At that time, any one that died either in the Medical Center or the Veterans Hospital was released to the funeral home from the large walk-in cooler located in the VA morgue. In fact, all the police calls or coroner cases were sent there as well for autopsy.

This Saturday afternoon the Mizzou Tigers were set to play Kansas State at Faurot Field. The stadium is located just across the street from the "Twin Towers of Death," as we commonly called the Medical Center and Veterans Hospital complex.

It was about an hour to game time, and the streets surrounding the hospital and stadium were packed with rowdy fans, some more obnoxious than others. I was riding shotgun in the hearse. Back then, we used the old clunky hearse that had once done double duty as an ambulance. The thing was extremely large and very morbid looking. In fact, it bore a strong resemblance to the Ghostbuster hearse. There was no mistaking our mission that afternoon.

Darryl drove as we crept our way through the black and gold-clad crowd. It was a nice late October day, so we had the windows down in the hearse. We slowed down to make the turn into the parking lot adjacent to the morgue entrance. About that time, a rather rude and perhaps slightly drunken fan leaned into Darryl's window and yelled, "HEY!! WHO DIED?"

Darryl didn't miss a beat. He looked the drunken fan right in the eye and coldly answered his irreverent question, "YOUR MOTHER!" The drunken fan looked quite stricken, and Darryl rolled his window back up and proceeded on to the morgue entrance.

I learned more than how to pick up a body out of the VA morgue that day. I learned how to handle a
Death Call Heckler! Thank you, Darryl.

Traveling Bra

The first 3 months into my first funeral job, I was still living at home with my parents. I was still in the hazing phase of my employment. One afternoon, my dad was out in the garage when I carefully backed my pickup down the driveway and tucked it against the house. I noticed him staring at the back of my truck as I finished parking it.

I was headed into the house when he pointed at the tailgate and gave his trademark knee-slapping, big laugh. I couldn't fathom what was so funny until a closer look revealed the ladies' brassiere carefully dangling from the tailgate handle. Yes, I had driven the 5 miles home in 5 o'clock traffic sporting a bra on the tailgate. Those boys. Anything for a laugh.

I got a place of my own a couple months later but didn't have a washer and dryer yet, so I would just take my basket of dirty clothes to work and drop them off at my parents' house afterward.

The next time I picked up my laundry from my mama, the traveling bra was lying on top of the folded clothes. My mama wanted to know if I knew whose bra it was. Yes. I had been burned twice by the same bra. As I returned it to our clothing stash at the funeral home, I wondered where and when the bra would turn up next. Hopefully, on a needy deceased.

Don't Forget the Paperwork

One of the most difficult tasks of taking care of the paperwork for a death that occurred in the teaching hospital was getting a signed death certificate that was properly filled out in black ink by the attending physician or resident. If everything was not correct the first time, it took days of calling and tracking down and waiting to get a properly-completed death certificate.

In the other hospitals, you could simply take the bad one, along with a typed corrected one, to their office and wait while the doctor just signed his or her name to it. I was so proud the day I had picked up a body at the Medical Center, and it was accompanied by the Holy Grail - a properly-signed death certificate in black ink. It was only when I got back to the funeral home that I noticed it was missing the resident's license number. After a couple of attempts to reach the resident, I gave up in despair. Because it was a natural death and everything else was proper, I went rogue and filled in a number that I knew by heart. Maybe some of you older fans of Hee Haw will recognize the number I "assigned" to the resident. Yup, BR-549. I hope there is a statute of limitations because that happened over 30 years ago. I altered no facts. Just assigned the future doc a cool license number.

Handle with Care

I was on vacation in Florida when I called my dad to check in. I was so proud of the fact I had just swam in the ocean that I didn't think to consider that he had done that and much more during his WWII Army days in the South Pacific. He listened patiently and then told me what had happened at the funeral home during my absence. I was glad I was out of town. It seems that his brother was at a funeral when the pallbearers arrived at the grave. They had just removed the casket from the hearse when one entire handle fell off. That effectively turned the casket into a 400 pound suitcase as the casket hit the asphalt parking lot. No one was injured, but the shock was very traumatic to the family who witnessed this debacle.

When I returned to work the following week, I got the full story from the unfortunate director in charge of this funeral. The quick-thinking director summoned enough help to load the casket back into the hearse. It was quickly returned to the funeral home where the undertakers went into pit crew mode. They placed the decedent into another casket, loaded him back up, and proceeded with the burial. A quick phone call to the casket company gathered an apology and an offer to replace the defective casket. At no cost, of course. The manager let the casket company say their peace and then told them what was actually going to happen.

"You are going to start by paying for this family's entire funeral expenses." "But. but," they stammered. "And then you had better hope they do not decide to sue us!!" They told the manager to return the broken casket and the defective handle. The manager knew enough to hold on to that important piece of evidence just in case it did come to trial. Lucky for the funeral home and casket company, this happened about 35 years ago when people were much less litigious. The family settled for the paid funeral expenses and apology. Good thing the casket's seal held and the body didn't pop out as well.

You can do everything in your power to make things go well, but you cannot control defective materials. I did feel sorry for the casket rep because he faithfully came around every couple of weeks to try to earn our business back. Finally, after a year or so when we were for sure we weren't going to get sued, we gradually introduced his products back into our showroom.

Slam That Door

I had been at my new job about 3 months when I drew the first complaint against the funeral home from Thanacap. Thanacap was a liaison between the National Funeral Directors Association and consumers. It was the place where the public could register complaints against funeral homes, and Thanacap could decide the outcome.

We had just completed the funeral of a young lady, and her father came to the funeral home to collect the potted plants and register book. I told him that they could only be released to her husband as he was the legal next of kin. Then it got ugly. "I paid for this (expletive deleted) funeral. Now gimme my (expletive deleted) plants. NOW!" I politely told him again that I could not release them to him without permission from the deceased woman's husband. "Now you listen here you (expletive deleted), you gimme my (expletive) plants. NOW! Or I'm gonna make you wish you had, you sorry (expletive)!"

Now I was just a 24 year old kid, but I wasn't gonna stand there and take a cussing from anybody. Grieving or not. To defuse the situation, I "helped" him out the door and said, "Whatever," as I slammed it in his face. He stalked off and I thought that was the end of it until the funeral home received the letter of notification from Thanacap about the way this gentleman was mistreated.

Luckily, we all know how legal government red tape works, and 38 years later I still have not received my comeuppance for my unprofessional and boorish behavior. I have had a lot of time and many more years of experience to think about how I handled this encounter. With the maturity and wisdom that decades bring, I must say that if this incident happened today I would have probably…. still slammed the door in his face. Bless his heart.

Casket 101

Batesville Casket Company. You have seen their trucks running up and down the highways. Perhaps you have seen them in a town where you live. Nice shiny, white trucks with a green tree imprinted on the side.

One of the selling points for Batesville is the fact that they promise to plant a tree in a national forest in honor of each and every deceased whose family chooses a Batesville casket. I am very proud of the fact that Roller went out of their way to honor every aspect of their pre-paid plans. If the casket wasn't available or was discontinued, they made sure to replace it with at least equal to or better than the original.

Early on in my career, one of the embalmers was making arrangements with a family. It came time to show them the caskets. He was explaining the differences in price and quality but made sure to tell them that "Batesville Casket Company will bury a tree in a national forest in honor of your father." Huh? The family was puzzled and rightly so."How or why in the world would someone bury a tree? For any reason?"

Yup. He meant to say they would plant a tree. My guess is that they actually just stuck a twig in the ground that would become a tree in the next 20 years. Maybe…Batesville still has three manufacturing plants in the USA and one in Mexico.

The solid copper caskets come in brushed copper finish or a choice of various painted colors such as white or light blue.

Although it is obviously a family preference, if I am gonna shell out the big bucks for a copper, I want it to shine like a new penny. If you are gonna throw some paint on it, you might as well buy a 20 gauge with swing bar hardware. Save yourself a couple or three thousand bucks. Probably more than you wanted to know about the last thing on earth you would want to buy.

A Bad Break

One cold day in January of 1998, I was carrying groceries into the house. The way our house faced, there was one particular patch of ice on the sidewalk that would partially melt and refreeze
for days. I had successfully dodged it and closed the back hatch. Just as I was warning my wife about the sidewalk, "Hey! Be very careful about that ice patch..." I slipped and braced for a fall. I locked my arms and both elbows crunched into my arm bones with the force of my full 275 pounds behind them.

I guess I was in shock because I kind of crawled into the house and sat on a chest as my arms dangled helplessly from my shoulders. A quick trip to the ortho doc revealed I had broken both elbows, and the only way to heal was a double sling, pain meds, and time.

For two weeks, I was basically paralyzed from the waist up. I couldn't feed myself or perform any chores that required use of either arm. The pain meds constipated me, so I needed bathroom assistance after a laxative. I was slumped against the door jamb, arms hanging down like useless appendages while my wife bravely attempted the clean up. And wouldn't you know it? She was a lefty. I can tell you that a diamond wedding ring will put you up on your toes if it scratches a tender area. Try to get that image out of your mind if you can.

After the two weeks, I was able to return to the funeral home but not really do anything. After 4 weeks, I felt I could be useful again. My first warning that all was not well was when I turned the steering wheel, and a sharp pain radiated from my elbow to wrist. My next test was at the nursing home when I tried a removal. The deceased was a little old lady. I wrapped her in the sheet and scooped both arms under her to lift her onto the cot. I watched in disappointment as my lift went about a foot off the bed, and my hydraulics gave way. I had to ease her back down and slide her over on a body moving board. The good news is that in a couple more weeks the bones had mended, and I was good as new. Kinda. The bad news is that the way they healed I kind of walked like Popeye the Sailor Man. Arms slightly cocked outward.

Return of Chet

Arranging a funeral isn't rocket science. Take care of the family. Listen. Gather information. Gently guide them through their choices. Listen. Become their emotional sponge. Eye contact is important. A light touch. Listen. Let them tell their story. Put yourself in their shoes. Treat them like family. Assure them as you walk them to the door that everything is under control. Express your sorrow for their loss. Then sit down for the follow up and checklist. Call the grave digger. Call the vault company. Call the preacher. Call the church.

E-mail the obit to the newspaper and the radio station and their hometown paper in Missoula, Montana, and half a dozen papers across the country. Scan the pictures for the DVD.

Mock up and proof the memorial folders and then print them. Get the death certificate started. Call the hairdresser. All that stuff happens when the family leaves. Most directors have OCD and do not rest until all these preliminary chores are completed. Most directors.

Roll back the years to 1985. Chet was drinking his coffee. We had his funeral set up in the chapel and ready to go.

"Hey, Chet. The cemetery called and said the vault hasn't been delivered yet."

Chet glanced over his newspaper. "Uh oh." Only Chet. He then proceeded to make 3 phone calls back to back. "Uh, yes. I need a concrete box delivered for a 1 pm service. Uh huh. Today. Yes. 1 pm today. Thanks!"

Next call went to the organist. "Uh, yes. Could you play for a funeral service at 1 pm? Uh huh. Yes. 1 pm today. Thanks!"

His final call went to the preacher. "Yeah. Uh, Jack? How's it going? Good. Heh heh. Well, I need you to preach a funeral. One pm. Today. Yes, 1 pm today. All right. Thanks!" Only Chet. His 3 phone calls took 10 minutes total and snatched his funeral from the jaws of disaster. He calmly went back to his newspaper. Only Chet.

A Slippery Slope

Concrete ramps are the best invention since the wheel in facilitating the removal of human remains from the service entrance of a hospital. However, an uncovered ramp plus ice can turn a routine call into a potential lawsuit.

Mark tried to talk the widow out of following him to the van that wintry evening. She insisted because after 40 years of marriage, she just couldn't bear to be apart from her Oscar. She not only wanted to accompany him to the van but wanted to catch a ride as well to the funeral home.

Mark had carefully dodged all the slick spots on the ramp on the way in and was now trying to ease his way back down with a loaded cot and a fresh widow in tow. The cot hit a patch of ice and slid down the ramp until it hit a parking block and collapsed the heavy end. Oscar slid off and lay on the ramp covered only by his skimpy hospital gown. The hospital gown did its job well and left Oscar's entire backside exposed. His wife took in the horror show and promptly fainted. Mark quickly called 911.

The EMTs were already at the hospital, so they arrived in record time. They immediately tried to revive Oscar until Mark pointed out that Oscar was beyond repair, and it was his wife that needed their expertise. Mark got Oscar loaded back up with help from an EMT. The wife was treated and released.
The whole sorry event became a cautionary tale for each new generation of undertakers. I don't recall if Oscar was charged for the failed jump start.

Faux Foot Follies

I don't remember where or how or even why I procured the bloody-looking, fake severed foot. The first use of it came when I slammed it into the trunk of a hideous, yellow-colored 74 Ford Maverick.

I thought the foot hanging out of the trunk was a hoot. The wife called that sedan the "Yellow Dog." I bought the car from a coworker for $600 and actually got to keep the foot hanging out of the trunk until I went to pick her up from her job at State Farm in Columbia. She discovered it, didn't quite find the humor in it that I did, and banished the foot. She didn't find the charm in the old yellow Ford either and banished it as well.

I sold the car for $600 to a fellow with no arms. He actually reached into his shirt pocket with his foot and pulled a checkbook out of his pocket with a couple of toes. He flipped the checkbook onto the floor. He then grasped a pen between his big toe, and the piggy that went to market and wrote the check.

But back to the foot. I next put the hideous-looking foot in the medicine cabinet at home in the guest bathroom. My thought was that when some nosy guest was going through the undertaker's medicine cabinet, they would see the bloody, severed foot and holler. That foot followed me to Arkansas. It wound up in a cabinet in the back room of the funeral home. I forgot to gather it when I collected my cardboard box of stuff on my last day. Just a heads up. If you find a stray foot back there, boys or girls, it's mine. I've got a little girl now that would just love to carry on the family tradition of practical jokes.

Two Weekends with Bernie

The patriarch of a prominent Columbia, Missouri family succumbed after a lengthy illness. He was taken into our care. The first clue we had that he was gonna stay awhile was when the funeral home owner told the embalmer to use a higher index embalming fluid and hit him hard.

One of his sons was on a safari in Africa and wasn't expected back in the area for another week or three. Mr. Jones was a slight old gentleman and wouldn't take up much room, so we covered him with a sheet and left him on a spare cot. A couple of days went by, and we ran out of space in the prep room; he was moved to the back hallway for another 2 or 3 days.

It became very inconvenient to try to wheel other guests past him so we moved him into Charlie's office. Charlie was out of town for a couple of days and it worked out well until Charlie returned and didn't want to share his napping area with Mr. Jones.The embalmers would check him every couple of days to see if he was dehydrated and needed any more moisturizing cream on his face.

After a week had gone by, we started to get used to our new guest. Other guests came and went, but Mr. Jones stayed. We even moved him back into the prep room for a couple of days until it filled up again. He spent a night or two in the old freight elevator as well. You just never knew where he was going to find lodging.

Eventually, the big game hunter returned to Columbia, and we were able to have the funeral and burial for his father. Mr. Jones didn't look too bad for having spent his last 2 and a half weeks after death above ground in a funeral home. He actually looked pretty good and was not shop worn at all. If we had kept him another couple of days, we would have had to put him on the payroll or given him our extended stay rates.

They Don't Sit Up

O.K., Friends. I think it's time we have the talk. I think we know each other well enough by now. So let us maturely and accurately discuss a thing or two that does not happen after death. Do you think I would have spent almost 40 years in the funeral profession if bodies just sat up during their ride to the funeral home or on the prep table? Come on now.

I have heard all kinds of stories from people who knew someone that had a cousin whose uncle's nephew had a brother that worked at a funeral home one time and had a body sit up on them. I am fixing to bust that myth once and for all. It simply doesn't happen. At least, it never happened to me. And if it did, I would have headed the other direction post haste, not to return.

Had such an incident occurred, I would have had to blame it on very poor embalming :). OK. Bodies don't sit up. They can poop. And they can pee. But Nossir. They don't sit up.

My next point is that I have worked at four different funeral homes and have never seen a ghost either. I did experience an "incident" the night my mother died. She was up in Missouri about 4 hours away from me at the time. It was more of a feeling than an apparition. But again I have made it 64 years without the pleasure of actually seeing a "haint."

My dad had slept in cemeteries in the Philippines during his Army days in WWII, and he said that was actually the safest and most peaceful night's sleep he ever had while overseas. He taught me at an early age that the dead can't hurt you. It's the live ones you have to look out for.

Front Porch Bandits

Deviate rocking chair thieves!! Robbie and I had moved to rural Arkansas to enjoy the wonderful small town atmosphere and be closer to her folks. Good native Baxter countians. This was God's country where a fellow could pee off his porch at night without violating a city code or two.

The boys at the funeral home were good people, and life was good. I enjoyed my shiny new job at the local funeral home and the rural tranquility of North Central Arkansas. My peaceful and innocent sanctum was shattered the morning I was backing out of my driveway and noticed that some deviate meth head had violated the sanctity of my domestic tranquility by stealing not one but both of my comfortable handmade wooden rocking chairs right off my front porch. They were there when I got home last night but gone by morning light.

I was seething and taking this loss quite personal. I had to get to work, so I decided I would call the police after I clocked in.

I parked in the back of the funeral home and let myself in the back door off the carport. I headed up the hall to the front office and came upon a scene out of Norman Rockwell. A couple of the embalmers (and I am gonna use their real names because of their shameful act), Brad and Todd, were sitting. And rocking. In the funeral home lobby. In MY chairs. They couldn't wait to tell me how they had parked down the street and crept by cover of darkness to my front porch. They had even peered in at my wife and me on the couch. They then each hoisted one of the heavy rockers on their respective shoulders and snuck away almost falling in the hideous ditch that bordered my front yard. The case of the missing rockers was solved. That was when I realized that I was one of the boys and would fit right in.

Down But Not Out

One Saturday morning I was on my way into work. I got behind a white SUV that was all over the road. He crossed over the center line and then went dangerously close to the ditch. I was only a minute or two from the cemetery entrance, so I decided to pull in there and make the call to the Sheriff's Office to get this guy off the road before he killed himself or someone else.

Who gets THAT drunk basically before the day even begins? Just then the SUV pulled into the cemetery ahead of me. Great! He realized that he was drunk and has decided to take himself off the road.

As I wheeled around the funeral home, I noticed the SUV had attempted a landing out back by the dumpster. At least he was stopped, but he had driven about 5 feet past the parking lot into the cemetery. It was only as he was struggling to exit the vehicle that I realized it was my weekend partner at the funeral home. Dick.

I ordered Dick to stay in his Blazer while I fetched the first call van. The way he was driving I feared he needed to lay down on the cot for his trip to the hospital. I was overjoyed it wasn't drug or alcohol induced, but you don't mess with dangerously high or dangerously low blood sugar.

By the time I brought the van around, Dick was sitting in a daze on the ground by his vehicle. "I told you to stay in the Blazer until I could get the van around!" Dick just gave me his weak smile and shook his head."I mumble mumble cars wash service." Translate that incoherent statement to "I have to get those cars washed before the service today!" Good, old conscientious Dick. He declined the offer of the cot, and I managed to load him into the passenger seat.

The hospital was only 5 minutes away, and I procured a wheelchair and checked him into the ER. Dick is still working part time at the funeral home. I would have to agree with Al, another tough old bird when he said that Dick was the best partner he ever had. Sure glad I didn't have to sic the laws on my old buddy that day.

Elvis Has Left the Building

Graceland. Robbie and I were in Memphis and of course had to tour Elvis's mansion. My first impression was that there are much larger homes right here in Mountain Home. Guess doctoring and lawyering pay more than entertaining. Elvis put his wife, daughter, parents and an extended crew of cronies and hangers on up in that relatively small home for such a world-class legend. While the other folks on the tour were gazing at his living room and stairway up to his bedroom and bathroom, I had different thoughts.

I thought about how he died in the bathroom directly over my head. My next thought was how in the world they removed the larger-than-life body of Elvis down that stairway. As we ended the tour, filing past the graves of Elvis, his parents and twin, I learned that he had originally been buried in Forest Hill Cemetery in Memphis beside his mama. After failed attempts by grave robbers, the bodies were moved to their permanent home at Graceland. By the way, if you are ever in Memphis, you should stop at the Civil Rights Museum located in the old Lorraine Motel where Dr. Martin Luther King, Jr. was murdered. You can see the exact spot on the balcony where it happened just outside the room he stayed in.

Back to the story. My 15 minutes of Elvis fame came a couple years later when the general manager of the funeral home in Arkansas introduced me to "the man that was a pallbearer for Elvis." The gentleman had been one of the fellows who was present at the disinterment in Forest Hill Cemetery back in 1977. Yes. I got to shake the hand of the man who touched the handle of the casket of Elvis. And I didn't even get a T-Shirt.

Eternal Safe Deposit Box

You know that folks get pretty sentimental when it comes to what they put in the casket with their precious deceased family members. Grandkids' pictures. Old love letters. Love letters written the night of the visitation. Bibles. Cartons of cigarettes.

Stuffed animals. Children's drawings. Photographs. All kinds of jewelry. Liquor bottles. Well, we didn't find out about that one until the casket was tipped to carry it upstairs into the church, and the bottle rolled from the foot to the head of the casket. Someone had tucked it under the metal frame that holds the mattress. Luckily, it didn't break. Ballcaps. Baseballs. Footballs. Golf Clubs. Cowboy hats. Fishing lures. Bowling trophies. Novels. Masonic Aprons. Transistor Radios. Horse Trader Magazines. Small hand tools. Urns containing the cremated remains of beloved pets. Toys.

The most heartbreaking are the toys and stuffed animals placed in children's caskets.:(. You name it. If it will fit, we will put it in there. I had always understood the sentimental part of this ritual, but the point became much more personal to me when my wife died.

At 44, she was much too young and her lingering death shattered me. My brother and sister-in-law had given her a nice quilt a week or two before she died. She was always cold, and the quilt was a nice gesture. The day of the funeral as I kissed her forehead, I tucked that quilt up under her chin before I closed the casket. Now I know on a
purely logical level "she" wasn't cold and would never suffer the discomforts of her disease again. But the grieving side of me decided she was cold and needed that blanket. It brought me a little more comfort as I prepared to return her earthly remains back to the earth. So I want you to know that it is more than OK to bring anything that will fit in that casket. We understand, and we really do care.

Settle That Estate, Boys!
This little dead time story comes compliments of my daddy. He has been gone 27 years, but I can remember a lot of the stories he told us kids.

Before we had the internet and cell phones, kids actually listened to their parents. I am sure glad I did. My dad grew up during the Great Depression on a farm, and one of the neighbors had 5 or 6 sons. He was a widower, and their sole source of heat was an antique wood stove placed in the center of the living room which also served as the kitchen and one partial bedroom. On especially cold nights they would feed that stove until it got red hot. When it reached dangerous levels, the dad would holler to his sons, "She's too hot, boys! Fetch her outside!" That was their cue to run a long pole through the top and carry it outside like they were moving the Ark of the Covenant.

The dad died when the boys were in their 20's and 30's. There was no will, and no will was needed. After the modest burial, his estate was settled by a knock down, drag-out fight that lasted for hours until the boys had determined who got what.

Punches were thrown and feelings were hurt, but in their own rough way, I think these boys condensed a year's worth of grieving into that one no-holds-barred fight. Dad was buried and the estate was settled without benefit or cost of a lawyer. I don't recommend this method of estate planning for everyone, but it worked for them.

Colonel's Secret Recipe

Lazarus. He's that old boy that Jesus raised from the dead. In 40 years, I had probably heard that story at least 4O times between church and funerals. The basics is that Lazarus, the brother of Mary and Martha, took ill suddenly. He was dead about 4 days. Jesus felt such compassion for these grieving ladies that he decided to raise him from the tomb.

I was sitting outside the chapel during a funeral service and was halfway listening to the message when apparently the preacher went rogue and started telling the story of Lazarus from his MOV Bible. You know. The "My Own Version." My ears perked up when the preacher got wound up and channeled

Colonel Sanders. He said these words to his captive audience, "Now, they had prepared Lazarus after his death. He was wrapped up in eleven different herbs and spices. After 4 days they was much afraid of the powerful staunch and smells. But Jesus said to Lazarus, 'you come on out of there.' And he come out dragging all them grave clothes with him. Jesus told them to unwrap him and let him go." Well, I guess that is one way to present that story.

After my initial shock and amusement, I was astonished to listen as that preacher tied everything together at the end and wound up giving a very comforting message to the family. After that funeral, I could never read those verses or hear that story again without picturing Lazarus wrapped up in the Colonel's secret recipe.

Let's Play the Family Feud

It's time to play the Family Feud. Daughter number one had brought out a couple of earrings and a diamond ring for her mom to wear during the visitation and funeral. When we closed the casket for the last time we made sure to remove all the jewelry and return them to daughter number one.

At the graveside service after the last amen, daughter number two came up to me and asked where her mama's diamond ring was. I pointed to daughter number one and said 5 words that sparked a hair pulling, wrestling on the ground, first class graveyard brawl. "I gave them to her."

"But Mama always promised that ring to me! That's mine and that ?!$&@ of a sister ain't gonna screw me out of it!" That was my cue and the other director's cue to exit stage left and hide behind the tent. As we hid there, the fight raged on. Finally, the vault company man took down the tent, and we lost our hiding place.

As the casket was lowered into the ground, the scuffle had simmered down into a cuss fight. Precious memories. How they linger.

Another Family Feud story comes from a fellow director. He was working in Springfield and was driving the family limo. Normally, you hear nervous small talk, but the back end was ominously quiet. The quiet was shattered by a commotion in the back seat.

,At the next stop light, the back door flew open and the two sons bailed out kicking and punching each other. The driver pulled to the curb as the fresh widow yelled at him to stop the fight. Any cop will tell you how dangerous it is to come between family. He simply waited until the boys got it out of their system and then proceeded on.

Guess who drew the complaint on that service?
Yup, the director who didn't stop the fight. Yes. Funerals can bring out the best and also the worst in people.

Gold Diggers

"I want daddy's gold tooth!" Fellow directors, how many times have you heard this request during a cremation arrangement? Or even a traditional burial arrangement?

Somewhere along the line, folks came up with the notion that funeral homes were knocking out gold teeth and making a "killing" (sorry not sorry) on the profits. I worked at 4 funeral homes, 2 of them with on-site crematories, and we never ever removed any gold teeth or gold caps nor gold crowns. The only item ever removed from bodies, and that is with expressed written permission of the next of kin, are pacemakers (the batteries blow up from the intense heat) and silicone breast implants (the silicone melts and gunks up the heat brick floor).

I was making arrangements with a lady who was very suspicious of the funeral trade anyway. "I want Dad's gold tooth before you cremate him!" I told her that we do not remove teeth, and if she wanted that procedure done, she would have to hire a dentist. She decided to kick it up a notch and asked me for the name and phone number of a dentist willing to come to the funeral home to extract the tooth. I gave her the information, and the next evening the dentist showed up and pulled the tooth. I don't know what he charged her for the dental house call but am pretty sure it cost her more than what the little dab of gold was worth.

After cremation there are all kinds of orthopedic remnants that have to be disposed of. Titanium Knees. Titanium Hips. Assorted surgical screws and pins. These are all collected in a common metal can for recycling or burial. One day, I was raking out the crematory, and a pair of charred hemostats fell into the collection tray. My first thought was some careless surgeon had left these in a body. This notion was quickly dispelled when an embalmer admitted he had used them to clamp the sheet closed around the rather large individual and had misplaced them.

How Do You Wish to Take Care of This?

Impecunious. Broke. Flat busted. Penniless. Financially challenged. Once in a while, I had to face a family who had no money to pay for a funeral. I understand that most of the time, death comes suddenly and at the worst of times including financially. That being said, most funeral homes will work with a family. And that being said, here are a few options. The "government" will not pay for a funeral. Social security will pay a surviving spouse $255. The county will not pay for a funeral. And here is a tip. Do not come into the arrangement office claiming you are broke and then take extended smoke breaks.

If you absolutely do not want cremation, some funeral homes will finance the funeral after a credit check and down payment.

Most funeral homes will also take insurance assignments. That means your life insurance will pay the funeral bill first and then release the balance to your family. There is no law that requires embalming. If you insist on traditional burial, and money is an issue, just choose no embalming and the least expensive casket. This choice does limit the viewing to just yourself and immediate family because of public health issues.

If you choose cremation, just get the direct cremation option. You can have a service anywhere, even your home. Computer savvy friends can make brochures. Cremated remains can be buried or scattered from the utility urn that comes with the cremation. Don't have the thousand bucks? Go Fund Me. Use your social media accounts. Nowadays there are many more options.

When I started back in the 70's, the financial policy was we would take half down and the rest now. I just want to give the undertaker's side of this. We cannot repossess a buried casket. We cannot hold cremated remains hostage. Nor would we. Funeral homes provide a valuable service and must be paid to stay in business.

Bubba Ain't Gonna Like This

Christmas Day 1997. Darryl and I had made it through the holiday with only a nursing home call the previous night about 10 pm. I had just decided after a big nap to plow through the remnants of the big family dinner for round two when we caught the residential call.

Apparently, the patriarch of the family had died after a lingering and painful illness. Two of the children were there to greet us as we entered the modest home.

I made the introductions, and the frail daughter introduced herself and her sister. She then exclaimed, "Bubba ain't gonna like this!" Hmmm. "Who is Bubba and where is he?"

Apparently, Bubba was the son who had been drinking most of the day. He had stepped out to walk to the 24 hour Quick Sack around the corner to obtain more liquor. The daughter again confirmed the fact that "Bubba ain't gonna like this!"

Daddy had died while Bubba was on his liquor run. And he wasn't gonna like this. There were 3 reasons why Bubba wasn't gonna like this. Either the fact that his daddy died. Or the fact that he died while Bubba was on his liquor run. Or the fact that his daddy died on Christmas Day. Or a combination of all three. Darryl and I put the removal into the fast lane because we didn't want to have to deal with an upset and liquored-up Bubba.

We took the father into our care and hastened to the removal van. Darryl got the back hatch closed. I got in the van, and Darryl jumped in the passenger side. I started to buckle up when an angry-looking fellow clutching a brown paper sack came stumbling up the street. I dropped the seat belt and started the van.

We were halfway down the street when Bubba made it to the now fatherless house. Darryl and I looked at each other and said those prophetic words simultaneously. "Bubba ain't gonna like this." And he didn't. But by the time we saw him again, he had a few hours to sober up and help his sisters complete the arrangements.

Raymond

Our latest apprentice from the local mortuary school was a man in his fifties. Funeral service attracts a wide variety and age group of prospective undertakers. Both men and women. This gentleman had a varied career path and decided to give funeral service a try. We were on our first call together at a boarding house. We entered the building and were greeted by a couple of cats. The call went well.

"Raymond" was wonderful help and handled his end of the cot like an old pro. I got the preliminary information from the family and set a time for the arrangement conference. We wheeled the deceased man out onto the front deck and had just closed the door when I heard a familiar song. The words were changed up, but "Bohemian Rhapsody" was being sung by Raymond as we wheeled the gentleman away. In honor of the cats, he channeled Queen and sang these words, "I'm just a purr man from a purr family…" I told him as quietly as my shocked voice could muster, "Raymond! You can't be singing on a death call! That's a no no!" He just grinned at me and looked a little sheepish.

A few weeks later, I was at the front of the chapel with a family for their first viewing. Now this is a nervous and somber time when you want to make sure everything is just right. It is like treading through a minefield of emotion and hoping not to set off any explosions of grief-fueled anger.

The family looked pleased when I could hear someone whistling a sprightly tune in the front entrance. The tune was in tune and kinda catchy but very inappropriate in the current setting. I excused myself and ran. Not walked. I ran to the front and confronted Raymond. I said, "You can't be whistling like that when a family is viewing." He just gave his sheepish grin and said he didn't realize he was whistling. I guess when you are happy and you know it, sometimes you just can't contain it. Ask my wife and daughter. My creative outbursts and joyful noises oftentimes go unappreciated around those two. I know I have overstepped the bounds when I hear my 7-year-old holler my name in 3 syllables, "DAD UH E!" Oh. Back to Raymond. He has a good heart and went on to get his funeral director and embalmer's license.

You Never Know What You Are Gonna Get

Coroner calls are like a box of chocolates. You never know what you are gonna get. Raymond, my partner on this call, was chatting away making a lot of small talk on the way to the house. I was mainly listening because I was thinking about what we were in for. I don't know how long the old boy had been dead, but you could smell him from the porch. I took their word because my smeller is impaired.

The coroner was on the scene because the death was unattended, and the decedent was far enough gone they were going to need an autopsy to determine the cause of death. I was gloving up and turned to give Raymond some gloves but could see through the window that he was out by a tree puking in the yard.

The coroner sounded like a photographer on a modeling shoot. "OK. Turn him this way. Good. Good. Now roll him on his stomach." He made sure there wasn't a knife hanging out of him.

"Lift his left arm and bend it this way." This went on for at least 10 minutes. I had an up-close view of the maggots as they did what they do. I think a couple were doing the "Macarena." Several had formed a conga line. A few were doing somersaults while the rest wiggled and jiggled. I finally grew weary and asked the coroner if he had enough snapshots.

"Just a couple more," he said. I had seen the movie before and was ready to wrap things up before the maggots put their sights on me. The coroner helped me place the deceased in a body bag and helped me load him into the van for his trip to a cooler clime.

After we had tucked him away in the cooler, the coroner asked us to retrieve the gentleman's wristwatch. Raymond drew the short straw. I would much rather just buy a new watch. Just saying.

Sneak Attack

Death calls come anytime of the day or night. Usually if a call came after midnight, the director on call would place the body in the cooler so a fresh embalmer could attend to it first thing in the morning. I had made a removal around 10 pm, and when I returned, I called Mark to give him the option of embalming it. He was still up and opted to just come on in and get it done. The next morning he was drinking his coffee and nursing a large bump on his forehead. The very dickens!

"What happened to you, Mark?" He said when he entered the darkened basement by the prep room, he was jumped and attacked. We knew that people were stealing embalming fluid out of prep rooms. Apparently, soaking cigarettes in the formaldehyde produced some kind of enhanced buzz. Luckily for us the assailant was solo. It was, however, a sneak attack. Mark had stepped on a carelessly-placed garden rake, and it cold cocked him just like in the cartoons. In the darkness, he said it came out of nowhere and smacked him between the eyes. He fought it into submission and then realized what had happened. He used some of the prep room cosmetics to mask his encounter before his arrangement conference that morning. More fodder for the obligatory monthly OSHA safety meeting.

Wrong-Way Roley

Old retired guys. Seems like nobody wants them except funeral homes. Give us your elderly, your retired, your sit around the house that you want to sit around someone else's house. Again I can say these things because I have joined the ranks.

Back in Columbia, we had a retired preacher who was a perfect fit for the job of funeral assistant. Mature, great sense of humor, and an ability to instantly bond with anyone in any situation.

Jim Roley had done countless funerals for us, worked numerous visitations and made a few road trips. On this day, his task was to take a burial 2 hours north to a small country cemetery. Because the family knew the way to this remote cemetery, we had Jim follow them as they left the funeral home. They drove a white Ford pickup with a camper shell. This was in the primitive days before cell phones. A few miles out of Columbia, Jim fell behind and lost the family. Luckily for him, he remembered the white Ford pickup with the camper shell. He spied it in a few miles and commenced to following it. And following it. And following it. The 1 pm burial time came and went and no Jim.

Finally about 1:45, Jim was pulled over by a sheriff's deputy. Jim leaned out the window and asked if there was a problem. The deputy informed him that if his cargo was headed to Olivet Celestial Cemetery, there was a BIG problem. The family was beyond irritated and had called law enforcement to see where their dead papa was. Yup. Jim had been following the wrong Ford pickup. Thirty minutes later - actually an hour and a half late for the graveside service, Jim pulled in.

I would like to report that the family was heartened that Jim hadn't been in a car wreck or had broken down somewhere. But I can't. An angry mob greeted Jim. This mild-mannered minister told me later that the family cursed him something awful and had used some REAL bad words. Poor Jim. He got back in the saddle and lived to work many more services for us but was forever known thereafter as "Wrong-Way Roley."

D.D. Grazier

D.D. Grazier. A polite, old, frail gentleman had lost his wife and came in to make the funeral arrangements. It was Mark's turn, and he sat down with D.D. to get everything set up. Mark asked the preliminary questions for the death certificate and the obituary. It took awhile because D.D. would answer a question and then sort of stare off into space.

Mark had to coax each fact out of D.D. Mark then started explaining the general price list. Started is the key word. "Well,

Mark. It's time for my tea and cookies. I must leave now, but I will return this afternoon."

Mark was incredulous. "Are you sure since you are here, you don't want to go ahead and finish the arrangements?" D.D.was adamant. He insisted on leaving but did return later that day as promised to finish the arrangement conference. The funeral and burial went well. About a week later, Mark went to the annual Oddfellows Bean and Cornbread fundraising dinner. He had just sat down when he heard a familiar voice.

"Well, hello, Mark!" D.D. was sitting there and proceeded to introduce Mark to his cronies. "Fellows. This is Mark, my undertaker." Just like Mark was his plumber or lawyer. He then finished the embarrassment with the following announcement made loud enough for the entire room to hear. "DON'T WORRY, MARK! I WILL BE IN NEXT WEEK TO PAY MY FUNERAL BILL!" All eyes in the room fell on the greedy undertaker who was pestering the poor old widower for his money. D.D. Grazier. The old coot was a real hoot.

Can You Start Now?

In my working years, I am proud to say that I was never fired from a job. Every job I quit was with the attitude instilled in me by my dad. "I was looking for a job when I found this one, and I will find another one."

I was between jobs and looking when out of the blue, my friend Dennis called me and said Memorial was looking for help. "I am not a salesman." I had seen an ad for them looking for a cemetery salesperson. Dennis assured me it wasn't a sales position, and I secured an interview the following Saturday at 2 pm. I chatted with the owner for about 15 minutes, and he said I was hired and agreed to pay me what my last job paid.

As I left, I asked him when I started. "We have a visitation at 5 pm. Can you be back in a suit by 4:30? And by the way we need you to shave that beard." I didn't mind losing the beard. I had only grown it while I was out of work for a couple of months. I was back and working the door at 5 pm that day.

The first visitor asked to use the restroom. I had to hunt for it myself. In the hasty hiring, I wasn't even given a tour of the building. I had trouble closing up that night because in a funeral home, there are numerous lights and hidden switches.

I was finally heading out the back door when Mark, one of the embalmers, was heading in. He was there to embalm a body and asked me who I was and why I was there. I told him I was the new funeral assistant and I was going to have to shave my beard. His reply told me I was at the right place. He gave me a deadpan look and said, "Aww that's O.K. They don't let me wear women's clothing here either."

I soon obtained my funeral director's license and stayed there for 15 years until Dennis opened his own funeral home and took me with him.

How Many Pallburiers Do We Need?

Pallbearers. I have heard them called many things. Whether you call them pallburiers, polar bears, or casket bearers, they are a vital part of the funeral and burial.

I have seen funerals on TV and movies where 6 strong men, all of the same height, carry a casket out of a church on their shoulders. I have never seen how they get that casket up there.

In my funeral career, all caskets were carried by the handles with as few as myself and the gravedigger or as many as 8 folks with 3 on each side and one on each end. Some families are blessed with enough nieces and nephews and grandkids to carry out this task. And yes, it is perfectly fine for someone of the female persuasion to join in. I found that it was the last thing I could do for a loved one. I helped carry both parents and my first wife to their final resting places. In the real world, you don't always have access to 6 physically fit gentleman that can heft 400-500 pounds shoulder height and then balance the load perfectly down stairs and into a hearse. In the real world, you hopefully have 6 folks that can carry the casket by the handles at waist level. And I am talking lifters here. Not leaners. It isn't fair to burden 4 borderline pallbearers with a couple that not only can't lift but use the casket as a walker.

Some of the hazards of pallbearing include but are not limited to: a long distance from hearse to grave; uphill carry; downhill carry; gopher holes; ice-covered ground; level grave markers; casket flowers sliding off; tripping on poorly-placed artificial grass.

Honorary pallbearers. If your loved one has friends you would like to acknowledge or an abundance of grandchildren, you can get them immortalized on the funeral program by making them honorary pallbearers.

No pallbearers? No worry. Cemetery or vault company staff will usually pitch in and help the hapless director. In my 4O years of funerals, we never had to leave someone in the hearse.

No Justice for the Jogger

Sunday afternoon at the funeral home. If there were no funerals, it was a good time to catch a nap.
This Sunday afternoon, the nap was interrupted by a coroner call. It seems there was a deceased young lady found just off the popular jogging trail in southern Columbia. I was allowed to drive the removal van on the trail to the location. She was located just off to the side of the trail. The medical examiner had made his preliminary exam and released her to me for transport to the VA morgue for an autopsy.

As I loaded her remains, I heard that she had been stabbed to death. In the following days, the sad details came out. A juvenile claimed that she had called him a racial slur, so he stabbed her to death. This was back in 1985. A human life isn't worth much more these days either. Maybe even less. I find it very sad that something as innocent as a jog on the trail could escalate into a violent end-of-life situation. I find it even sadder that the kid who ended her life was simply placed in juvenile detention until he turned 21. If he hasn't killed again, he is enjoying his middle-aged life by now.

Our justice system certainly failed this young lady, and I fear it hasn't gotten any better since the 80's. That call affected me deeply. You just don't forget senseless and violent loss of innocent life.

Old Highway 40

During slow times at the funeral home, I found a fascinating pastime. Old accounts from the 30's and later were kept in ledgers in a fireproof archive room. I enjoyed reading the archaic obituaries that included the cause of death: he looked at his watch and said, "It's 5 o'clock, boys. Then he fell dead from an attack of apoplexy."

They not only contained graphic causes of death but also included home addresses of the deceased. If death was due to a gruesome car crash, it invariably included a newspaper clipping complete with an uncensored photo of the accident scene. Bodies thrown through the windshield or otherwise ejected. I was fascinated by these and began to notice a pattern.

Old Highway 40 was just a two-lane road running from Kansas City to St. Louis. Add a 60 MPH speed limit. Mix in cars and trucks made of American steel with V8 motors. Subtract seat belts and smaller collapsible steering wheels. Lose the air bags. Add in primitive and undermanned law enforcement. The result is horrific head-on automobile crashes.

According to my amateur "research," these fatal accidents occurred quite regularly on that stretch of road before I-70 pretty much made Highway 40 obsolete by the mid 1960's. Those old archives
are a treasure trove depicting life and death from a simpler time.

Can You Dig This?

Pre-paid funeral plans. I encourage them. They really do take a huge burden off surviving relatives. You can even put aside money towards expenses that cannot be frozen such as sales tax, obituaries, grave opening, minister and musician fees and death certificates. Death certificates were another discussion starter.

"How many death certificates do you think you will need?" I would explain what they needed them for. "Oh. Just get me a dozen." I would let them know the state charges $10 per certified copy. "Oh. Just get me one. I can make all the copies I need." I would gently let them know that no one would accept a Xerox copy.

Eventually, after much discussion, we would determine that they actually needed 4 certified copies. I guess the biggest disappointment families faced when learning that the prepaid plan didn't cover everything was when we came to the cemetery expense. This was back in the 80's. $500 ??? Just to dig the grave??? They always had a buddy or a cousin who knew someone with a backhoe that would dig it for less. Cemetery rules would not allow outside diggers. It got so bad that the cemetery had brochures printed up trying to justify why it cost so much to dig the grave. Those brochures didn't help their case much and were discontinued soon after they were introduced.

Another shock was the sales tax. "You mean they are taxing stuff that is just gonna be buried in the ground?" Any tax shouldn't be shocking nowadays. They even tax social security retirement. Yes, they tax money that has already been taxed. I highly recommend pre-paid funeral plans, though. I know some old ones from the 60's that sold for $650 back then and are worth $5000-$6000 now.
Just some things to think about when you run out of things to think about.

St. Louis or Bust

One of the owners of Parkers, Charlie loved taking road trips. He also enjoyed company on those trips. I had a date set up for Friday night and had been looking forward to it for a couple of days.

About noon that Friday, Charlie decided he wanted to take a cremation to Valhalla in St. Louis. He asked if I would go with him. Back then you had 2 options for such a rare procedure. Drive the 130 miles to Kansas City or drive the 125 miles to St. Louis.

It was about 4 pm when we finally left Columbia. Charlie loved to discuss places of note along the way. Places such as the old Fletcher Brothers Farm or a home where he had made a removal. He pointed out all the cemeteries as well. Trouble is he "pointed" with the hearse. He would get to talking and motioning, and soon the hearse would veer toward the left or right. Wherever the attraction was. Along about Kingdom City, 20 miles east of Columbia, he decided that we needed to stop in at Gaspers, a popular truck stop, for supper. He ordered fried chicken and I ordered a burger.

Twenty minutes later, Charlie said, "They must be catching that chicken." Five minutes later, he observed, "They must be butchering that cow."

By the time our meals came and were devoured, it was about 6 pm. Charlie, being the executive, made an executive decision. "Well, it's too late to head to St. Louis. Let's just make this trip tomorrow."

I arrived back at the funeral home too late to reschedule the date. We unloaded the hearse and went our separate ways. I didn't dare try to set the date for Saturday night. Charlie might take another notion for a road trip.

I miss those old days. Life was a lot slower, and people were more patient. People were willing to wait for their cremated remains. They came back in the mail in a couple of weeks. Now, if the paperwork is in order you can get them back the same day if you don't mind the heat radiating from the utility urn.

Tour Guide

Robbie can tell you that I have a portion of my mind that stores useless facts and trivia. I also can pretty much recall the places and circumstances of the dozens of house calls I have been on in my almost 40 years of funeral service.

Typical conversations in our vehicle. "I picked up a guy that shot himself in his bathtub in that house. Very considerate. Easy clean up. Oh by the way, see that ditch beside the road on the way to that house? That's where that serial killer dumped the salesman." Robbie - "Um Hmm"

"Got a guy off the toilet in that house. See that 2 story brick? Big old boy - we had to put him in a body bag and slid him down the stairs." Robbie -"Hmm."

"Got a lady out of the back bedroom of that trailer. Man those hallways are too narrow for a cot." Robbie - "Yup."

"See that loading dock behind the high rise? They wouldn't let us take bodies out the front door so we had to lower them from that dock in back." Robbie - "Well, I'll be."

"Got a guy that killed his wife and then himself up above that store there on the left. Quite a mess." Robbie - "How awful!"

"A semi truck ran over a concrete truck that slowed down there at that intersection. The driver didn't have any visible injuries. Must have suffocated." Robbie - "You mentioned that before."

"This exit ramp is the one that car was stopped at when the semi plowed into the back and killed that guy and his son." Robbie - "You mentioned that before."

"That hotel is the one where that guy hung himself." Robbie - "You said he shot himself." "No that was that other guy at that other motel." "I buried my dad's cousin in that cemetery." Robbie - "Uh Huh."

"That's the church we forgot the church truck at and had to delay the funeral." Robbie - "What is a church truck?" And all that was just in Columbia.

I have a whole new set of places to point out from my Arkansas days. "See that Volunteer Fire Dept? That's where I had to turn around when I missed the turn to Promiseland Cemetery." Robbie - Inhale and big sigh. Jaci: "I didn't see the cemetery. Where's the cemetery?" Good girl.

Music

I had an uncle that passed away in 1975. He was a country music fan, and my aunt wanted some country songs played at his funeral. The organist tried. Bless her heart. The closest thing she could come up with was "One Day At A Time." Just doesn't hit you in the feels when played on the organ.

In 2005, when my wife passed away, I played Diamond Rio's "One More Day," Hank Williams's "Beyond the Sunset," and "I Bowed On My Knees" by the Gaither Vocal Band. Those last 2 songs would be considered religious, but that is not my point. My point is that with the technology we have these days, it is easier to play songs that will stir emotions and memories instead of simply giving a break in the preaching.

I am all for religious songs at a funeral. However, a funeral service is not a worship service. I believe you can have both secular and religious songs. Acknowledge and praise God our creator! Give Him honor for blessing us with the life of the deceased. But also play something that will coax those tears to flow. Grief held in just festers. Let those emotions come out and let the long, and sometimes never ending, healing begin.

I was blessed at my mama's funeral to have my cousin and her daughter accompanied by my cousin's husband on the guitar. Their close family harmony on "Old Rugged Cross" triggered the silent tears for me. Live or You-Tube.

Please don't underestimate the power of music at a funeral or memorial service. Was Dad a big band era fan? Throw on the Glenn Miller greatest hits CD as a prelude and postlude. Mom loved Conway Twitty? Burn some of her favorites on an audio CD and crank it up at the visitation. Let me throw out a few suggestions for the service itself. Both sacred and secular - "I Can Only Imagine," "Holes in the Floor of Heaven," "I'll Fly Away," "When I Get Where I'm Going," "Old Rugged Cross," "Peace in the Valley," "Wind Beneath My Wings," "Freebird," "The Dance," and probably the most requested "Go Rest High."

BS Detector

I drove the 20 minutes to our funeral home in Ashland to relieve Chet so he could get a supper break. He was on the front porch of the funeral home and exchanging stories with a handful of the assembled guests.

Chet pulled me aside for a private conversation. "I need you to go inside and call my pager. I need that thing to go off in about 5 minutes." I didn't know what he had in mind, but I couldn't wait to see what mischief he had planned.

In about 5 minutes I called the number to his pager. I could hear him say something and then just a bunch of raucous laughing. When the visitation settled down, I caught Chet and asked him what delinquency I had contributed to. "Wahl. Wallace Jackson was telling one of his whoppers when my pager went off. Those old boys wanted to know what that was. I just told them that's my B.S. detector that he had set off."

OK one more Chet story. He told me that the light "bob" in the elevator shaft needed replacement, and he wasn't tall enough, even on a chair, to change it. I grabbed a funeral home folding chair and climbed on. As I reached the "bob," I touched the hanging fixture and fell off the chair as I got the tar shocked out of me.

Chet had tears in his eyes - he was laughing so hard. "It needs more than a new light bob I guess." When I quit hurting, I had to admit it was funny. Everyone needs a coworker like Chet. He kept things real. Real funny.

Bowls of Blood

We caught the police call about an hour after lunch. Perfect timing. David and I entered the Section 8 apartment building, and luckily the policeman was standing outside a door on the first floor. Upon entering the apartment, we saw a cereal bowl full of blood sitting randomly on the floor. There were also ashtrays, saucers, and other assorted dishes full of blood. Blood had splattered the floor in various places as well. The decedent was naked and lying on a sofa.

The first thoughts that came to my mind were satanic sacrifice or some other kind of occult practices. The whole scene looked kind of witchy to me. Kind of made the hair on my arms stand up. We wrapped the emaciated victim in a sheet, and as we moved him to the cot, the sofa wobbled like it was off center. David and I lifted the sofa and found a less scary but equally sad cause of death. The sofa was high centered on all the empty half pint and pint bottles of vodka. There must have been at least 20 empty bottles scattered under there.

This poor gentleman literally drank himself to death. Due to the years of alcohol abuse, he had finally eroded his esophagus until a blood vessel burst, and all he could do was vomit blood. We will never know why he chose to fill all the dishes with his blood. I can sum up the entire call in one word. Sad.

That Turkey

Visitations are what you make of them. Greet the visitors, look them in the eye, hang up their coat. Make them feel at home. You know. My funeral casa is your funeral casa. Throw all the rules out the window when working one with Chet.

"Got me a new turkey call Donkey." Donkey was one of his pet names for me. Get it? Don Lee. Donkey? "That's cool, Chet!" "Been wanting to try it out." We spied a lady getting out of her car. Chet couldn't resist. He inserted that diaphragm call into his mouth and waited until she was about 5 feet from the door. "SPOOT SPOOT!!
SCREE SPOOOOOT!!!"

I looked at Chet with amazement and then watched that old gal looking carefully around for incoming butterballs. I managed to stifle my laughter until I got her coat hung up. Thankfully, Chet saved his turkey mating dance until she was safely ensconced in Parlor B.

OK. One more Chet story. Frank Sapp could fall asleep anywhere and at anytime. Add a 40 minute funeral service to the mix, and he was always out by the end of the opening prayer. Chet and I were dismissing the crowd after a particularly dry service. When Chet got to Frank's row, progress was halted because Frank was sprawled flat out into a deep sleep.

Chet looked at me, and I knew what was next. It was like watching a dump truck going down I-70 with the dump bed fully raised just waiting to hit the next overpass. I watched in amusement as Chet grabbed Frank and shook him. Frank let out a cry of fear and promptly fell out of his funeral home folding chair. Chet and I helped him up and out, and the rest of the folks filed out. Chet behaved himself the rest of that day. At least, I don't think that's the same day he found a large oak tree in the back of the cemetery to pee behind.

Losing a Child

Of all the pain of searing loss I believe that losing an infant or child is the absolute worst. As a parent, I believe that losing a child, one that you would gladly trade your own life for, is a loss that I cannot even start to fathom or imagine.

During my career, I saw families that bonded closer together and families that were torn wide apart by the loss of a child. My advice (for what it is worth) is after a stillborn or infant death is to let mom hold the child as long as she wants. Have a service and then cremate. Yes, you read correctly. Cremation with the cremated remains returned in a small pastel color urn. My reasons for this are simple yet complex. Young couples that lose children have the option to bury in a local cemetery. However, think ahead. Two years. Five years or Ten. If the couple are even still together, the chances of them staying in the same town forever, especially when burdened with the unspeakable grief, are questionable. With cremation, the remains can stay with Mom and/or Dad throughout the years. Cremated remains in a nice urn can easily weather divorce or relocation.

Also, a lot of funeral homes will not charge for infant services. Usually, there is a fee from the cemetery for an infant space with grave marker. Cremation allows the parents the freedom to keep the earthly remains of their precious child. This is just my opinion, and it is neither right nor wrong. Roller provided a sheet bronze cube painted pink, blue, or white at no cost to the already-burdened family. Just something to consider if the unthinkable ever happens. Explore your options.Trust your funeral director. They are on your side.

Time Marches On

Mary Street was an ideal place to start a family back in 1952 when my parents bought the little bungalow. The price of $5000 would get you a 2 bedroom and 1 bath home. The paucity of space was made up for with an abundance of love.

Some of the best memories of my life were made in that little house. By the 1990's after my dad died, my brother and I took turns with the lawn care. I would glance fearfully at every car driving slowly down the street just bracing for the drive-by shooting or errant bullet from a drug deal gone bad. We could never convince my mama to move because she was there first. By the end of the 90's, my childhood home would be within the epicenter of 5 murders.

One hot and humid July day, the crackhead across the street from her back-fence neighbor snuck in the back door and suffocated and kicked her to death so he could get some drug money. He stole her car and a weed eater.

He was arrested the same day because he decided to drive by the crime scene and gawk at the gathered law enforcement and coroner team processing it. A year or two later in November on election night, a drugged-up thug shot and killed his step father and aunt in the house across the street from my mama. He then chased his girlfriend into the street where he shot and killed her. She was still holding her 2 year old and 6 month old as she collapsed against my mama's fence.

Sometime around that time, a drug deal went bad on the street that runs north of Mary Street. The victim's car traveled through a back yard until it crashed into a house across the street from my mama's house. That makes 5 murders within 50 feet of my boyhood home.

Mom is gone now. My home now is Mountain Home, Arkansas. Also known as Little Chicago because of all the northerners who retire here. Columbia, Missouri, my hometown could also be dubbed Little Chicago because of the high homicide rate. To quote Merle Haggard, "Are the good times really over for good?"

Suits Me Just Fine

A couple of the funeral homes I worked for either gave a clothing allowance or bought the directors and embalmers a suit once a year. O.K. The suits were "aight." By "aight" I mean they were average suits that kinda fit, and that was fine. The $100 suits were very much appreciated. However and there is always a but. They were certainly not worth the price tags that came attached to them. $295 for a pair of pants? $350 for the suit coat? Come on now. Somebody was getting some kind of tax write-off selling a $100 suit for 650 bucks.

My first disappointment came the day I put the $350 suit coat on. Being used to thrift store suits, probably donated by widows of freakishly large men, I had never encountered a pocket sewn shut on a new suit. I went to put my keys in the pocket, and it wouldn't open. Being young and suffering from a serious couth deficiency, I jammed my right hand into the pocket and yanked. The pocket came open along with about 6 inches of the coat. Yup. Ripped that sucker clean off.

In the funeral home's defense, those suits were purchased from a burial garment salesman. A burial garment looks like a suit, but that is where the similarities end. The pants are one size fits all stretch pants, and the coats are one size fits all as well. Easily tailored, in other words. Burial garments are quickly becoming extinct as more folks turn to cremation and casually dress their dead. T-Shirts, Polo shirts, flannel shirts, and overalls or jeans are the rule these days. Suits are fast becoming the exception. After almost 40 years of suits and ties, I myself prefer the comfort of T-Shirts and jeans and have instructed my wife to not throw a suit on Myra Mains. I kill me.

Cosmetics

One of the keys to a successful funeral is having the guest of honor "look natural." I can't even paint a wall without getting more paint on me than the wall. I never tried to apply cosmetics and always left that to the embalmers. Since I was a newbie, they would make me go to the Merle Norman store downtown and purchase the war paint. I was even given the dubious errand of purchasing women's hosiery and underwear in bulk at the Bargain Barn. I didn't mind those errands after getting over the shame and awkwardness. I even became an advocate of the dead, making sure underwear was available for all, whether the family brought it in or not.

Perhaps my lack of cosmetic skills came from watching Charlie in the early days of my career. He would stand back after the body was dressed and casketed and eye it very carefully. "He's not ruddy enough, men." "Ruddy" - meaning the corpse wasn't wearing the flushed red tones that Charlie sported. He believed that everybody should be the same color as the back of his hand. He would hold that hand next to the decedent's face and invariably determine that he or she was definitely not ruddy enough.

I guess subconsciously I carried that advice throughout my career and thus had trouble applying the Marvelous Mauve. Either that or I just couldn't bring myself to rouge a dead man's cheeks.

Lions, Bears, No Tigers

Finally - a story for you animal lovers. You know who you are. I will straight up admit that I am not a hunter. I prefer my turkey sliced thin out of the deli case. But since I have been in Arkansas, I have seen a couple of creatures that usually are confined to either a zoo or gathering dust in a Bass Pro Shop.

One Memorial Day weekend on a Sunday afternoon, I was sitting in the funeral home lobby discussing something with Dick and Hal. We were deep in conversation when I noticed a large, and I'm talking huge, black dog saunter past the window. Curious to see if the dog was gonna poop on the sidewalk, I opened the front door just in time to see the tail end of a black bear heading off into the cemetery.

I hollered for one of my buddies, and they confirmed that I had indeed seen a genuine Ursus Americanus. That sighting turned our conversation from Hal's Navy days during the Cold War of the early 60's to discussing our various theories as to why this particular Bruin chose to visit our neck of the woods.

Perhaps he went over the mountain to see what he could see. He was last seen on all fours heading down towards the crematory. Might have been a she, but we didn't see any Boo Boo bears.

Later that summer I had an encounter with another exotic creature. It was about 2:30 AM, and I was heading back from a death call to my home out in the boondocks north of town. I was turning onto my little dead end when I caught something out of the corner of my eye. The hair on my arms stood up as I watched the panther-sized "mountain lion" trot past my headlights, head and long tail hanging down as it headed for the pasture on the back side of my back fence.

I am not going to say it bothered me. Much. Because I was safely in my Escape and could park inside my garage. However, the "mountain lion" sighting certainly took the fun out of peeing off my front porch at night. Well that and the fact that some folks finally bought the homes across the street from me. But mainly the "mountain lion." I really thought it was a panther until I was told that there are no black panthers in Arkansas. Tell that to the panther. Believe it or don't. And I recommend you don't go outside in the dead of night in the woods around the Midway area of Baxter County.

Extraneous Accoutrements

In my almost four decades of funeral service, I accumulated quite a collection of funeral home stuff. I prefer the term "assorted extraneous accoutrements." My wife prefers the term "morbid junk."

The jewel of my collection is a cast iron scale model of a horse-drawn hearse complete with the horses and coffin. That would look so cool on our fireplace mantel. I also have a piece of folk art welded by a buddy who is now deceased. Six pallbearers carrying a casket. That thing is all metal and probably weighs 20 pounds.

It would look great as a centerpiece on my kitchen table, right? Robbie says wrong. I have a nice solid brass casket paperweight that has followed me around for at least 30 years. It would be perfect for any room or occasion, right? Robbie says wrong.

I have numerous hot wheels-sized hearses that would be beautifully displayed in the living room. I could even purchase a fancy lighted display case for them, right? Robbie says wrong.

I have a nice framed glass wall hanging of a hearse-drawn hearse. Would look good in any bathroom… Except ours. Or Jaci's.

My wooden casket pencil case with RIP on the lid is the perfect conversation starter. It would look great on my desk. If I had a desk. Or someone to start a conversation about it with. The good thing about being retired is I do seem to enjoy my own company. The downside is starting conversations with myself. Thanks for listening.

Epilogue

You have come to the end of this short collection of short recollections of my years as a funeral director. I hope these true stories have made you laugh and/or cry in the appropriate places. Life is limited. You can choose to be happy or not. I always tried to make any job I had a happy place. I guess the best advice I want to leave with you comes from the wisest man who ever lived, King Solomon, whose wisdom came directly from an answered prayer to God. Ecclesiastes 12:13 says, "Let us hear the conclusion of the whole matter: Fear God, and keep his commandments: for this is the whole duty of man."

Thank you for sharing my little corner of the world.